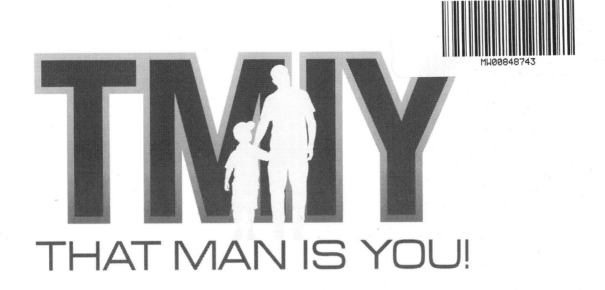

THAT MAN IS YOU!

The Spirit of Nazareth

PowerPoint Presentations

Paradisus Dei

HELPING FAMILIES DISCOVER THE SUPERABUNDANCE OF GOD

A Publication of Paradisus Dei · www.paradisusdei.org

SESSION 1
Apostles of a New Springtime

TMIY
THAT MAN IS YOU!
BECOMING A MAN AFTER GOD'S OWN HEART

Source: Craughwell, T., "Saints Behaving Badly: The Cutthroats, Crooks, Trollops, Con Men, and Devil-Worshippers Who Became Saints," Image, 2006, pp. 10-17.

We had an incredible year last year.

One of the highlights was the stories.

We met many saints and many scoundrels.

I have another one for you.

St. Callixtus: Pope and Martyr

- Sixteenth pope.
- Reigned 218-223AD.
- Merciful pope – allowed Christians who had committed mortal sin to do penance and re-enter the Church.
- Martyred either in popular uprising or thrown into a well.
- Buried in the "Chapel of the Popes" in the Catacomb of St. Callixtus on the Appian Way.
- Relics moved to Santa Maria in Trastevere.

Source: Craughwell, T., "Saints Behaving Badly: The Cutthroats, Crooks, Trollops, Con Men, and Devil-Worshippers Who Became Saints," Image, 2006, pp. 10-17.

St. Callixtus: Pope and Martyr

- Lived as a slave to Carpophorus.
- Carpophorus decided to establish a bank for Christians, especially widows so that their money would be safe.
- Places Callixtus in charge of bank.
- Callixtus squanders most of the money and embezzles the rest.
- Christian widows are destitute. Carpophorus is irrate.
- Callixtus flees Rome.

Source: Craughwell, T., "Saints Behaving Badly: The Cutthroats, Crooks, Trollops, Con Men, and Devil-Worshippers Who Became Saints," Image, 2006, pp. 10-17.

St. Callixtus: Pope and Martyr

- Callixtus is convicted of disturbing the peace, scourged and exiled to Sardinis to work in the mines.
- Marcia, the mistress to the emperor, receives permission to have all Christian prisoners released.
- Pope St. Victor I does NOT include Callixtus in list of Christian prisoners.
- Callixtus begs to be released. Returns to Rome.
- Pope St. Victor I and Carpophorus are furious to see Callixtus in Rome.

Source: Craughwell, T., "Saints Behaving Badly: The Cutthroats, Crooks, Trollops, Con Men, and Devil-Worshippers Who Became Saints," Image, 2006, pp. 10-17.

How does someone become a true scoundrel?

How does someone go from a scoundrel to a saint?

Welcome to Apostles of a New Springtime!

St. Callixtus: Pope and Martyr

- Carpophorus captures Callixtus on a boat in Portus.
- Carpophorus sentences Callixtus to hard labor – binding him to a gristmill.
- Wronged depositors beg mercy for Callixtus.
- Carpophorus releases him with the instructions to retrieve as much money as possible.
- Callixtus enters Jewish synagogue during the Sabbath prayer service and demands return of money.
- A riot ensues.

Source: Craughwell, T., "Saints Behaving Badly: The Cutthroats, Crooks, Trollops, Con Men, and Devil-Worshippers Who Became Saints," Image, 2006, pp. 10-17.

St. Callixtus: Pope and Martyr

- Pope Victor I places Callixtus in house well outside the city walls on the Appian Way.
- Callixtus is converted.
- He begins helping a priest, Zephyrinus.
- Zephyrinus becomes Pope, ordains Callixtus as a deacon and places him in charge of Christian cemetery on Appian Way – catacombs of St. Callixtus.
- Zephyrinus dies and Callixtus is elected Pope.
- Callixtus is known for tremendous mercy.

Source: Craughwell, T., "Saints Behaving Badly: The Cutthroats, Crooks, Trollops, Con Men, and Devil-Worshippers Who Became Saints," Image, 2006, pp. 10-17.

Apostles of a New Springtime

Fall Semester

- Get inside the head of some of the most interesting characters in Scripture.
- Dissects the issues involved on both the spiritual and natural level.
- Identifies the spiritual solution to the main issues.

The Tools at Our Disposal

The Three Wisdoms

- The best research from secular science (especially medical and social science).
- The teachings of our faith (based upon Scripture, Tradition and the teachings of the Magisterium).
- The wisdom of the saints handed down through the centuries.

Apostles of a New Springtime

Fall Semester

- Identifies the pathway traveled from sinner to saint.
- Provides an examination of conscience according to the 7 Steps of TMIY.
- Provides a framework to help men make progress in their spiritual lives.
- Helps men develop a spiritual plan-of-life.

We make a major transition for the Spring Semester.

Our goal is to hear and respond to the voice of God.

The Call of That Man is You!

- "Wherever you are in your spiritual life, Jesus Christ wants to encounter you right there … and take you further."
- "That Man is You! is about a personal encounter with Jesus Christ so that Jesus Christ can transform your life."

- We have begun a journey to become authentic male leaders.
- We must build this leadership on the Rock of Christ.

" Jesus Christ personally invited you to be here today. You said, 'Yes.' And I thank you. "

Apostles of a New Springtime

Spring Semester

- Considers the "call of God."
- Identifies the context within God speaks today.
- Provides 7 principles for discernment.
- Considers the discernment of St. Joseph.
- Provides the opportunity to respond to God's call.

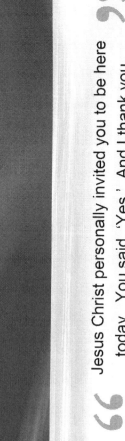
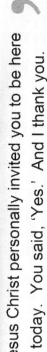

The Path of That Man is You!

Understanding the Three Roles of Men

- Year 1: We considered man in his relationship to God and sought to become a man after God's own heart.

- Year 2: Provides men the practical tools they need to become a man after God's own heart.

- Year 3: We consider man in his role as husband and seek to become the hidden face of Christ for our spouse.

- Year 4: We will consider man in his role as father and seek to transform men into the Revelation of God the Father.

The Vision of Authentic Male Leadership

| Moral Leadership
Personal Responsibility |
| Military Leadership
Clarity of Thought
Integrity of Action |
| Political Leadership
Foundation for Future |
| Economic Leadership
Foundation for Future |

Sacrifice
The willingness to pay the price.

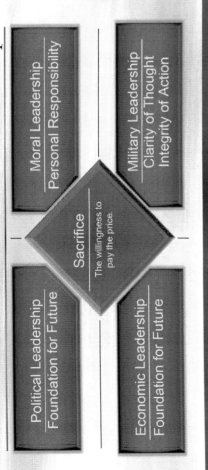

Small Group Discussion

Starter Questions

1. Who do you know that has radically transformed their life? How did they do it?
2. Who are you going to bring with you next week?

Next Week
From Saint to Scoundrel

" We are hungry for this as men and our lay men in particular have been starving for this. This is truly rich in what the Church teaches … The manifestations of God's presence happen suddenly, sometimes profoundly. There is a real ripple effect from this program in the lives of the men who attend it. "

Fr. Jim Gigliotti, TOR⊠ Arlington, Texas

The ways of men are mysterious.

Some men have everything ... and lose it.

The story of Josh Hamilton.

SESSION 2

From Saint to Scoundrel

TMIY

THAT MAN IS YOU!™

BECOMING A MAN AFTER GOD'S OWN HEART

Josh Hamilton: The Recovery

- Grandmother is the only one who will take him in.
- Dreams of fighting the devil.
- Crawls in bed with his grandmother.
- Goes through 4 years to rehab his body.
- Returns to MLB with Cincinnati. Traded to Texas.
- Has five consecutive all-star seasons: 2008-2012.
- Wins MVP in 2010.
- Legitimate triple crown threat.
- December 2012: Signs five-year $125 million contract with Anaheim Angels.

Source: Chen, A., Sports Illustrated, "The Super Natural," June 2, 2008.

Josh Hamilton: The Descent

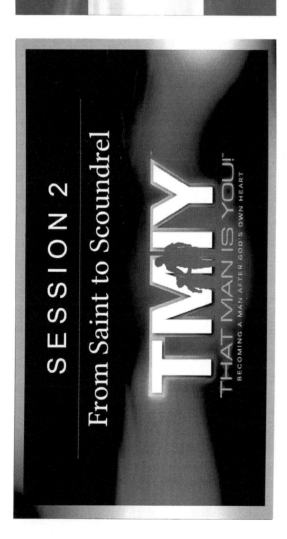

- Born May 21, 1981.
- High School Player of the Year. Throws 96mph. Bat speed 110mph.
- Overall 1st pick by Tampa Bay in 1999.
- Dominates minors; challenged to get a tattoo by Carl Crawford.
- Car accident in 2001 leaves him unable to play.
- Begins hanging out at tattoo parlor. Starts drinking, doing crack, blows bonus.
- "When I first got into drinking and using drugs, it was because of where I was hanging out, it was who I was hanging out with. You might not do it at first, but eventually, if you keep hanging around long enough, you're going to start doing what they're doing."

Source: Chen, A., Sports Illustrated, "The Super Natural," June 2, 2008.

Josh Hamilton: The Relapse

- Substantially below expectations for Angels.
- Only 31 home runs and 123 RBIs in two years.
- 2014 ALDS: Goes 0-13 as Angels swept by KC Royals.
- Needs offseason shoulder surgery.
- Has a fight with his wife.
- Writes himself a check to get cash.
- Goes to a strip club and does cocaine.
- Enters rehab.
- Files for divorce from wife.
- Traded to Texas Rangers.

How does someone with everything going for them sink so low?

Believe it or not, the precedent goes all the way back to the very first man.

The Dignity of the Human Person

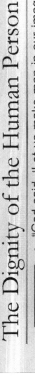

- "The Lord God formed man of the dust from the ground, and breathed into his nostrils the breath of life; and man became a living being" (Genesis 2:7).
- "The human person, created in the image of God, is a being at once corporeal and spiritual. The biblical account expresses this reality in symbolic language when it affirms that 'then the Lord God formed man of dust from the ground, and breathed into his nostrils the breath of life; and man became a living being' (Genesis 2:7)" (Catechism #362-363).

The Dignity of the Human Person

- "God said, 'Let us make man in our image, after our likeness ... So God created man in his own image, in the image of God he created him; male and female he created them" (Genesis 1:26-27).
- "Being in the image of God the human individual possesses the dignity of a person, who is not just something, but someone. He is capable of self-knowledge, of self-possession and of freely giving himself and entering into communion with other persons" (Catechism #357).

The Gift of Self-Knowledge

- Man is given the gift of intelligence were he can know himself and others – including God.

- "Man ... shares in the light of the divine mind ... His intelligence is not confined to observable data alone, but can with genuine certitude attain to reality itself ... The intellectual nature of the human person is perfected by wisdom and needs to be, for wisdom gently attracts the mind of man to a quest and a love for what is true and good. Steeped in wisdom, man passes through visible realities to those which are unseen" (Gaudium et Spes, #15).

The Gift of Self-Possession

- Man is given the gift of freedom (free will) so that he can make the gift of himself to enter into a communion of love.

- "God created man a rational being, conferring on him the dignity of a person who can initiate and control his own actions ... Freedom is the power ... to act or not to act, to do this or that ... By free will one shapes one's own life .... Freedom makes man responsible for his acts to the extent that they are voluntary" (Catechism #1730-1734).

The Gift of Interior Integrity

- Humanity is given the gift of interior integrity. The intellect and will are in harmony so that man does not experience an interior disorder.

- "The 'mastery' over the world that God offered man from the beginning was realized above all within man himself: mastery of self. The first man was unimpaired and ordered in his whole being because he was free from the tripe concupiscence that subjugates him to the pleasures of the senses, covetousness for earthly goods, and self-assertion" (Catechism #377).

The Gift of Communion

- "Therefore a man leaves his father and his mother and cleaves to his wife, and they become one flesh" (Genesis 2:24).

- "God created man and woman together and willed each for the other" (Catechism #371).

- "Man cannot live without love. He remains a being that is incomprehensible for himself, his life is senseless, if love is not revealed to him, if he does not encounter love, if he does not experience it and make it his own, if he does not participate intimately in it" (St. John Paul II, Redemptor Hominis, #10).

The Temptation of Humanity

The serpent was more subtle than any other wild creature that the Lord God had made. He said to the woman, 'Did God say, 'You shall not eat of any tree of the garden?' … You will not die. For God knows that when you eat of it your eyes will be opened, and you will be like God, knowing good and evil.' When the woman saw that the tree was good for food, and that it was a delight to the eyes, and that the tree was to be desired to make one wise, she took of its fruit and ate; and she also gave some to her husband, and he ate.

Genesis 3:1-6

Humanity had everything going for us.

Unfortunately, it doesn't last and we make a royal mess of everything.

The Darkening of the Intellect

- "For now we see in a mirror dimly … now I know in part" (1 Corinthians 13:12)
- "As regards spiritual faculties this deterioration consists in a darkening of the intellect's capacity to know the truth … Even after original sin, man can know by his intellect the fundamental natural and religious truths, and the moral principles …. One should therefore speak rather of a darkening of the intellect" (St. John Paul II, General Audience, October 8, 1986).

The Reality of a Fallen World

- "And the eyes of them both were opened: and when they perceived themselves to be naked, they sewed together fig leaves, and made themselves clothes. And when they heard the voice of the Lord God walking in paradise at the afternoon air, Adam and his wife hid themselves from the face of the Lord God amidst the trees of paradise" (Genesis 3:7-8).
- "Scripture portrays the tragic consequences of this first disobedience. Adam and Eve immediately lose the grace of original holiness. They become afraid of God … The harmony in which [Adam and Eve] had found themselves, thanks to original justice, is now destroyed: the control of the soul's spiritual faculties over the body is shattered; the union of man and woman becomes subject to tensions, their relations henceforth marked by lust and domination" (Catechism #399-400).

The Weakening of the Will

- "I do not understand my own actions. For I do not do what I want, but I do the very thing I hate" (Romans 7:15).

- "As regards spiritual faculties this deterioration consists in a ... weakening of free will. The will is weakened in the presence of the attractions of the goods perceived by the senses ... Even after original sin, man ... can also perform good work. One should therefore speak rather ... of a weakening of the will" (St. John Paul II, General Audience, October 8, 1986).

Damaged Communion

- "Your desire shall be for your husband, and he shall rule over you" (Genesis 3:16).

- "As a break with God, the first sin had for its first consequence the rupture of the original communion between man and woman. Their relations were distorted by mutual recriminations; their mutual attraction, the Creator's own gift, changed into a relationship of domination and lust" (Catechism #1607).

The Body Subject to Infirmity and Death

- "Because you ... have eaten of the tree of which I commanded you, 'You shall not eat of it,' cursed is the ground because of you; in toil you shall eat of it all the days of your life; thorns and thistles it shall bring forth to you ... In the sweat of your face you shall eat bread till you return to the ground, for out of it your were taken; you are dust and to dust you shall return" (Genesis 3:17-19).

- Man's material body will now decay and death.

The world is indeed now different. We all struggle with a darkened intellect, weakened will and disordered relationships.

We need to see what led us down this pathway.

To Lose the First Love

- "Adam wanted to be like God [but] without God" (St. Maximus the Confessor, Catechism #398).

- "I have this against you, that you have abandoned the love you had at first. Remember then from what you have fallen, repent and do the works you did at first, If not, I will come to you and remove your lampstand from its place" (Revelation 2:4-5).

A Strike at the Heart of Man

"Man, tempted by the devil, let his trust in his Creator die in his heart and, abusing his freedom, disobeyed God's command. This is what man's first sin consisted of. All subsequent sin would be disobedience toward God and lack of trust in his goodness."

Catechism #397

Small Group Discussion

Starter Questions

1. How do you struggle with doing things you really don't want to do?
2. Where do you need to increase your trust in God?

Next Week
From Scoundrel to Saint

This issue of the heart is very big.

We must remain true to our first love.

We will see that it returns again and again throughout this Fall semester.

Last week we considered the transition from saint to scoundrel.

Is it possible to make the journey from scoundrel to saint?

SESSION 3

From Scoundrel to Saint

TMIY

THAT MAN IS YOU!

BECOMING A MAN AFTER GOD'S OWN HEART

The Wanderings of St. Augustine

"So for the space of nine years (from my nineteenth to my twenty-eighth year) I lived a life in which I was seduced and seducing, deceived and deceiving, the prey of various desires. My public life was that of a teacher of what are called the 'liberal arts.' In private I went under cover of a false kind of religion. I was arrogant in the one sphere, superstitious in the other, and vain and empty from all points of view" (Confessions, Book IV, Chapter 1).

Source: St. Augustine, "Confessions," Trans. Chadwick, H, Oxford World's Classics, Oxford University Press, 2008.

St. Augustine

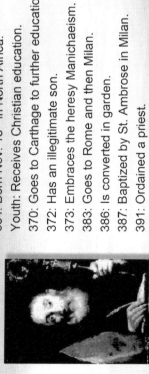

354: Born Nov. 13th in North Africa.

Youth: Receives Christian education.

370: Goes to Carthage to further education.

372: Has an illegitimate son.

373: Embraces the heresy Manichaeism.

383: Goes to Rome and then Milan.

386: Is converted in garden.

387: Baptized by St. Ambrose in Milan.

391: Ordained a priest.

396: Ordained bishop of Hippo in Africa.

430: Dies on August 28th.

The Conversion of St. Augustine

"A huge storm rose up within me ... Suddenly, a voice reaches my ears from a nearby house ... 'Take it and read it' ... I snatched up the book, opened it, and read in silence the passage upon which my eyes first fell: 'Not in rioting and drunkenness, not in chambering and wantonness, not in strife and envying; but put ye on the Lord Jesus Christ, and make not provision for the flesh in concupiscence.' I had no wish to read further; there was no need to" (Confessions, Book VIII, Chapter 12).

Source: St. Augustine, "Confessions," Book 10, xli Trans. Chadwick, H. Oxford World's Classics, Oxford University Press, 2008.

A New Way of Life

- "So under the three forms of lust I have considered the sicknesses of my sins, and I have invoked your right hand to save me ... You are the truth presiding over all things. But ... [I] wanted to have you at the same time as holding on to a lie ... Who could be found to reconcile me to you? ... Was I to beg the help of the angels ... Many have tried to return to you, and have not had the strength in themselves to achieve it."
- Abandons position in rhetoric.
- Lives a monastic life of fasting, prayer, good works and meditation on Scripture for 3 years.

Source: St. Augustine, "Confessions," Book 10, xli Trans. Chadwick, H. Oxford World's Classics, Oxford University Press, 2008.

Light from Above

- Augustine was walking on the seashore contemplating the mystery of the Blessed Trinity.
- He saw a young boy using a seashell to take water from the ocean to a small hole in the sand.
- He asked the young boy what he was doing.
- "I am trying to bring all the sea into this hole."
- "That is impossible my dear child, the hole cannot contain all that water."
- "It is no more impossible than what you are trying to do – comprehend the immensity of the mystery of the Holy Trinity with your small intelligence."
- Augustine paused and looked up.
- When he looked down, the boy was gone.

Source: Voragine, J., "The Golden Legends: Readings on the Saints," Princeton University Press, Princeton, NJ, 2012, pp. 502-517

Finding Union with God

"You were within me and I was outside, and there I sought for you and in my ugliness I plunged into the beauties that you have made. You were with me, and I was not with you ... You called, you cried out, you shattered my deafness: you flashed, you shone, you scattered my blindness: you breathed perfume, and I drew in my breath and I pant for you: I tasted, and I am hungry and thirsty ... When in my whole self I shall cling to you united, I shall find no sorrow anywhere, no labor; wholly alive will my life be all full of you" (Confessions, Book X, Chapters 27-28).

Source: St. Augustine, "Confessions," Trans. Chadwick, H. Oxford World's Classics, Oxford University Press, 2008

The transformation of St. Augustine has followed a pattern that has been well known in the Church from its earliest days.

The three stages of the interior life.

Rediscovering the First Love

- "O Lord, you have made us for yourself, and our hearts are restless until they rest in thee" (Confessions, Book 1, Chapter 1).

- "Late have I loved thee, beauty ever ancient, ever new, late have I loved thee!" (Confessions, Book X, Chapter 27).

Source: St. Augustine, "Confessions," Trans. Chadwick, H. Oxford World's Classics, Oxford University Press, 2008.

Purgative Stage: An End to Selfishness

- "He must increase, but I must decrease" (John 3:30).

- God must free us from our selfishness.

- "No matter how much individuals do through their own efforts, they cannot actively purify themselves enough to be disposed in the least degree for the divine union of the perfect love. God must take over and purge then in that fire that is dark for them" (St. John of the Cross, *Dark Night*, I.3.3).

Source: "The Collected Works of St. John of the Cross," trans. Kavanaugh, K., ICS Publications, Washington, 1991, pp. 366-367.

The Three Stages of the Interior Life

- Pseudo-Dionysius: 5th or 6th Century.
- Confusion with St. Dionysius converted by St. Paul and St. Denis of Paris.
- Writings on mystical theology.
- Very important Church Father in Eastern Orthodoxy and western medieval ages.
- "What we humans call the beatitude of God is ... full of continuous light and is perfect ... It is purifying, illuminating, and perfecting."

Source: "Pseudo Dionysius: The Complete Works," The Classics of Western Spirituality, Paulist Press, New York, 1987, "Celestial Hierarchy" 3.2, p. 155.

Illuminative Stage: From God's Perspective

- "When I was a child, I spoke like a child, I thought like a child, I reasoned like a child; when I became a man, I gave up childish ways" (1 Corinthians 13:11).
- Freed from selfishness, we see things in a new way.
- "In this new state, as one liberated from a cramped prison cell, it goes about the things of God with much more freedom and satisfaction of spirit and with more abundant interior delight ... The soul readily finds ... a very serene, loving contemplation and spiritual delight" (Dark Night, II.1.1.)

Source: "The Collected Works of St. John of the Cross," trans. Kavanaugh, K., ICS Publications, Washington, 1991, pp. 395.

Unitive Stage: Foretaste of Paradise

- "If a man loves me, he will keep my word ... and we will come to him and make our home with him" (John 14:23).
- "The ninth step of love causes the soul to burn gently ... The Holy Spirit produces this gentle and delightful ardor by reason of the perfect soul's union with God. We cannot speak of the goods and riches of God a person enjoys on this step because even were we to write many books about them the greater part would remain unsaid" (Dark Night, II.20.4.)

Source: "The Collected Works of St. John of the Cross," trans. Kavanaugh, K., ICS Publications, Washington, 1991, pp. 444.

The home at Nazareth.

For the past generation, the Popes have been identifying the perfect school to learn the spiritual life:

The home at Nazareth.

The School of the Gospel at Nazareth

"Nazareth is a kind of school where we may begin to discover what Christ's life was like and even to understand his Gospel ... Here everything speaks to us, everything has meaning ... How I would like to return to my childhood and attend the simple yet profound school that is Nazareth!"

Blessed Pope Paul VI
Address at the Basilica of the Annunciation
January 5, 1964).

The "Programme" for Third Millennium

- "To contemplate the face of Christ, and to contemplate it with Mary, is the 'programme' which I have set before the Church at the dawn of the third millennium, summoning her to put out into the deep on the sea of history with the enthusiasm of the new evangelization" (Pope John Paul II, *Ecclesia de Eucaristia*, #6).

- "Together with Mary, Joseph is the first guardian of this divine mystery ... one can also say that Joseph is the first to share in the faith of the Mother of God" (Pope John Paul II, *Redemptoris Custos*, #5).

St. Therese and the Way of Love

- "I know, O Mother full of grace, that you lived in great poverty in Nazareth. You did not long to leave it; no raptures, miracles or ecstasies lightened your life ... you chose to tread the everyday paths so as to show little ones the way to heaven."

- The little way: "I applied myself to practicing little virtues, not having the capability of practicing the great."

- The way of love: "O Jesus, my Love ... my vocation, at last I have found it ... my vocation is Love."

Source: Quoted in Longenecker, D. "St. Benedict and St. Therese—The Little Rule and the Little Way," Our Sunday Visitor Publishing Division, 2002, p.175

"Start of a Soul—The Autobiography of St. Therese of Lisieux," 3rd Edition, Translated by Clarke, J., ICS Publications, 1996, pp.159, 194

The Life of Nazareth

Holy Family at Nazareth	Paradisus Dei
1. The Niddah Laws on sexual purity (Cf. Leviticus 15:19ff).	1. Honor your wedding vows.
2. The separation of the Challah (Cf. Numbers 15:20).	2. Use money for others.
3. The Nerot Laws (Exodus 20:8).	3. Give God some of your time.
4. The angel is sent to Mary and Joseph to open their minds.	4. Set your mind on the things above.
5. Mary finds God in self.	5. Find God in yourself.
6. Joseph finds God in Mary.	6. Find God in other people.
7. The Christian home is born of mercy.	7. Make it easy to be good and hard to be bad.

Nazareth and the Spiritual Life

7 Steps of That Man is You!	3 Stages of the Spiritual Life	
1. Honor your wedding vows.	1. Give away your body.	Purgative Stage
2. Use money for others.	2. Give away your goods.	
3. Give God some of your time.	3. Give away your time.	
4. Set your mind on the things above.	4. Receiving illumination from God.	Illuminative Stage
5. Find God in yourself.	5. Union with God in self.	
6. Find God in other people.	6. Union with God through others.	Unitive Stage
7. Make it easy to be good and hard to be bad.	7. Ultimate union with God.	

Developing the Spirit of Nazareth

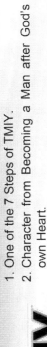

TMIY
THAT MAN IS YOU!
BECOMING A MAN AFTER GOD'S OWN HEART

1. One of the 7 Steps of TMIY.
2. Character from Becoming a Man after God's own Heart.
3. Spiritual Issue – tied to science.
4. State of TMIY men.
5. Spiritual Remedy.
6. Path to Success.
7. Suggested Examine.

It was in the home at Nazareth that Jesus "increased in wisdom and in stature, and in favor with God and man."

(Luke 2:52)

We need to follow him in his journey.

We need to enter into the "spirit of Nazareth."

Small Group Discussion

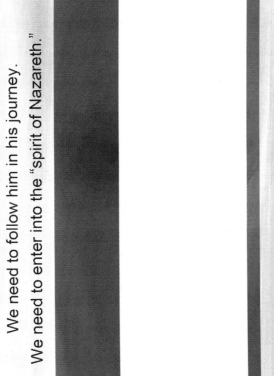

Starter Questions

1. Who do you know that has made the transition from scoundrel to saint?
2. Can you name the 7 Steps of TMIY? Have you tried to live them?

Next Week

Honor your Wedding Vows

Slide 1

We wish to "increase in wisdom and in stature and in favor with God and man."
(Luke 2:52)

We need to follow Christ in his journey to Nazareth.

Slide 2

Developing the Spirit of Nazareth

1. 7 Steps: Honor your wedding vows.
2. Character: King David.
3. Spiritual Issue: Lust/competing brain systems.
4. State of TMIY men: Very difficult issue.
5. Spiritual Remedy: Penance and mortification.
6. Path to Success: Strengthen will.
7. Suggested Examine: 10 questions on spousal union.

Slide 3

SESSION 4

Honor your Wedding Vows

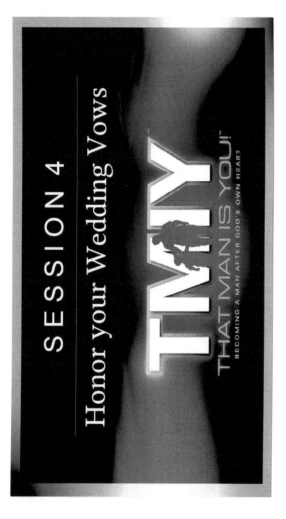

Slide 4

Nazareth and the Spiritual Life

7 Steps of That Man is You!

1. Honor your wedding vows.
2. Use money for others.
3. Give God some of your time.
4. Set your mind on the things above.
5. Find God in yourself.
6. Find God in other people.
7. Make it easy to be good and hard to be bad.

3 Stages of the Spiritual Life

1. Give away your body. — Purgative Stage
2. Give away your goods.
3. Give away your time.
4. Receiving illumination from God. — Illuminative Stage
5. Union with God in self.
6. Union with God through others. — Unitive Stage
7. Ultimate union with God.

A Man after God's own Heart

"[God] raised up David to be their king; of whom he testified and said, 'I have found in David the son of Jesse, a man after my heart, who will do all my will.' Of this man's posterity God has brought to Israel a Savior, Jesus, as he promised."

Acts 13:22-23

We're in the purgative stage.

"He must increase, but I must decrease."

John 3:30

The entire basis for the first year of TMIY – Becoming a Man after God's own Heart – was King David.

He's a good place to start.

Recovering the First Love

"

Have mercy on me, O God according to thy steadfast love; according to thy abundant mercy blot out my transgressions … Against thee, thee only, have I sinned, and done that which is evil in thy sight, so that thou art justified in thy sentence and blameless in thy judgment …. Create in me a clean heart, O God, and put a new and right spirit within me. Cast me not away from thy presence … O Lord, open thou my lips, and my mouth shall show forth thy praise. For thou hast no delight in sacrifice … The sacrifice acceptable to God is a broken spirit; a broken and contrite heart, O God, thou wilt not despise.

Psalm 51:1-17

"

The Life of King David

- Chosen by God and consecrated as King of Israel by the Prophet Samuel.
- Commits adultery with Bathsheba, who becomes pregnant with his child.
- Arranges for the death of Bathsheba's husband, Uriah.
- Takes Bathsheba for his wife.
- Confronted by the Prophet Nathan who tells David the parable of the two men.

Competing Brain Systems

- Attraction: Testosterone, caudate nucleus (reward center of brain), ventral tagmental area (VTA), dopamine (cocaine like substance); primacy of visual clues.
- Attachment: Oxytocin, vasopressin, dopamine, lateral septum (emotion), nucleus accumbens (reward/reinforcement), middle insula and anterior cingulate (perceptions of self).
- "Romantic love is primarily a motivation system … romantic love is distinct from the sex drive" (Helen Fisher).

Source: Fisher, H., "Why We Love – The Nature and Chemistry of Romantic Love," Henry Holt and Company, LLC, 2004, pp. 67-76; 104-110.
Accredo, B., et al "Neural correlates of longterm intense romantic love," Oxford Journals. Social Cognitive and Affective Neuroscience, 2011.
Fisher, H., et al, "Romantic Love: An fMRI Study of a Neural Mechanism for Mate Choice," The Journal of Comparative Neurology, 2005

Sexual Fidelity is an Issue

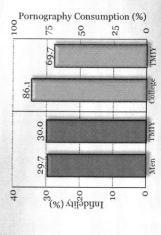

- Reported rates of infidelity has almost tripled since the 1920s.
- Approximately 30% of men admit to having been unfaithful to their wives.
- TMIY men report similar numbers.
- Almost 90 percent of college men view pornography.
- Almost 70 percent of TMIY men view pornography.
- Approximately 37.5 percent of TMIY men have visited a topless bar.

Source: General Social Survey 1972-2012
Carroll, J. et al, "Generation XXX: Pornography Acceptance and Use Among Emerging Adults, Journal of Adolescent Research, 2008 23: 6.
TMIY Internal Data.

What was the issue for King David?

Obviously, lust.

Let's go further – there are some interesting things happening in a man's brain.

Competing Brain Systems

- "The harmony in which [Adam and Eve] had found themselves … is now destroyed: the control of the soul's spiritual faculties over the body is shattered" (Catechism #400).
- Attraction System: Activates in less than one second when a man sees an attractive woman.
- Attachment System: Restructuring of the brain to form "pair bond" occurs over time.
- Romantic Love system to help moderate.
- If attraction system is left unchecked, men focus upon female body parts and process images as an object in the brain.

Source: Wang, Z, et al "Neurochemical regulation of pair bonding in male prairie voles," Physiology and Behavior, 2004.
Lykins, A., "Detection of Differential Viewing Patterns to Erotic and Non-Erotic Stimuli Using Eye-Tracking Methodology," Archives of Sexual Behavior, 2006.
Cikara, M., "From Agents to Objects: Sexist Attitudes and Neural Responses to Sexualized Targets," Journal of Cognitive Neuroscience, 2010

Recovering your First Love

- Think back to your wedding.
- Think back to the desires of your heart.
- I've talked to a lot of men. The vast majority truly wanted to be faithful to their spouse. They truly wanted to put her first. They truly wanted to be sacrificial. Those desires were not wrong. They were beautiful. Unfortunately, many of us have lost our first love.
- Perhaps we should work to recover it.

Man has disharmony within himself.

When it comes to sex, attraction runs way ahead of attachment.

✝ What is a man to do? Ascetical Practices.

Taming the Triple Concupiscence

- "All that is in the world, the concupiscence of the flesh and the concupiscence of the eyes and the pride of life, is not of the Father" (1 John 2:16).
- Concupiscence of the flesh: penance and mortification.
- Concupiscence of the eyes: charity.
- Pride of life: prayer.

Strengthening the Will

- "God created man a rational being, conferring on him the dignity of a person who can initiate and control his own actions ... Progress in virtue, knowledge of the good and ascesis enhance the mastery of the will over its acts" (Catechism #1730-1734).
- Forego morally neutral things you like.
- Do morally neutral things you don't like.
- Approximately 22% of TMIY men do penance on a weekly basis.

Building a Spiritual Plan of Life

1. Develop Intentionality
   - Entrust your purity to Mary and/or St. Joseph.
   - Reread/renew your wedding vows.
   - Make it tangible: carry a Rosary in your pocket; wear the Miraculous Medal.
2. Get the Grace Flowing
   - Attend Mass more frequently.
   - Go to Confession whenever you've fallen.
   - Increase Prayer – in general and at moment of temptation.

Building a Spiritual Plan of Life

3. Form your Mind Correctly
   - Turn off media.
   - Set appropriate filters on ALL electronic equipment.
   - Get information on The Theology of the Body.
4. Strengthen your Will
   - Give up something you really like: food, alcohol, watching sports.
   - Do things you don't like: food you don't like, take cold shower, turnoff A/C in car.

Building a Spiritual Plan of Life

5. Receive help and support from others.
   - Establish a buddy system: "Two are better than one … For if they fall, one will lift up his fellow; but woe to him who is alone, when he falls and has not another to lift him up" (Ecclesiastes 4:9-10).
   - Consider a 12-Step group.
   - Seek professional help.

Developing the Spirit of Nazareth

1. The Way of Love
   - ALWAYS speak to and about your wife with charity: "If anyone makes no mistakes in what he says, he is a perfect man" (James 3:2).
   - Sacrifice of your own desires to put those of the family first.
2. Ascetical Practices (Things you give up)
   - Food: Joyfully eat whatever is served; Take wife and children to restaurants they prefer.
   - Sports: Don't watch/participate in sports by self. Give time to family.
3. Ascetical Practices (Things you do)
   - Joyfully fulfill requests by wife and children for help.
   - Use time to be with family members in things they enjoy.
   - Give open access to all electronic equipment.

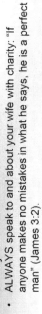

The Spousal Bond as Pathway to God

- "Joseph, son of David, do not fear to take Mary your wife" (Matthew 1:20).
- "Sacrifice and offering thou hast not desired, but a body hast thou prepared for me" (Hebrews 10:5).
- "Spouses are therefore the permanent reminder to the Church of what happened on the Cross; they are witnesses to the salvation in which the sacrament makes them sharers. Of this salvation event marriage, like every sacrament, is a memorial, actuation and prophecy ... Marriage is a real symbol of the event of salvation" (Pope John Paul II, *Familiaris Consortio*, #13).

Evaluation on Honor Wedding Vows

1. Have I been sexually unfaithful to my spouse?
2. Have I visited a "topless bar" or establishment where women are not fully clothed?
3. Have I viewed pornography or other sexually explicit materials?
4. Have I lusted after women or objectified my spouse?
5. Have I flirted with or given special attention to another woman?
6. Do I frequently argue or disagree with my spouse?
7. Have I withheld affection from my spouse?
8. Do I sleep in a separate bed from my spouse?
9. Do I go to bed at the same time with my spouse (one of you is not asleep before the other one comes to bed)?
10. Do we use contraception in our spousal union?

Infidelity – real or virtual – is just the starting point.

Our spousal union is called to lead us into communion with God.

I would suggest a 10 question evaluation.

Small Group Discussion

Starter Questions

1. What specific steps are you going to take today to take it to the next level on Step 1?
2. What were the desires of your heart when you got married? How are you going to live them?

Next Week
Use Money for Others

We wish to "increase in wisdom and in stature and in favor with God and man."
(Luke 2:52)

We need to follow Christ in his journey to Nazareth.

Developing the Spirit of Nazareth

1. 7 Steps: Use Money for Others.
2. Character: King Solomon.
3. Spiritual Issue: Greed/competing brain systems.
4. State of TMIY men: Very difficult issue.
5. Spiritual Remedy: Charity
6. Path to Success: Increase generosity.
7. Suggested Examine: 10 questions on finances

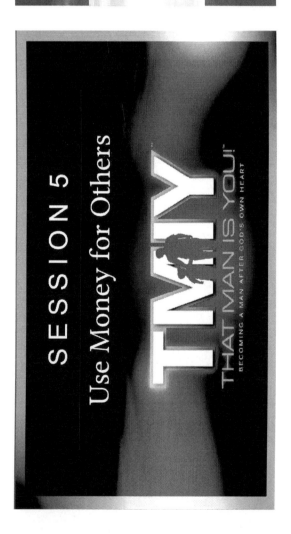

Nazareth and the Spiritual Life

7 Steps of That Man is You!

1. Honor your wedding vows.
2. Use money for others.
3. Give God some of your time.
4. Set your mind on the things above.
5. Find God in yourself.
6. Find God in other people.
7. Make it easy to be good and hard to be bad.

3 Stages of the Spiritual Life

1. Give away your body.
2. Give away your goods.   } Purgative Stage
3. Give away your time.
4. Receiving illumination from God. } Illuminative Stage
5. Union with God in self.
6. Union with God through others.   } Unitive Stage
7. Ultimate union with God.

The First Love of King Solomon

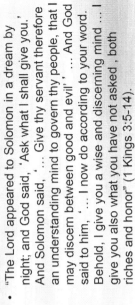

- Born approximately 1000 B.C.
- Second son born to King David and Bathsheba.
- "The Lord appeared to Solomon in a dream by night; and God said, 'Ask what I shall give you.' And Solomon said, '… Give thy servant therefore an understanding mind to govern thy people, that I may discern between good and evil' " … And God said to him, ' … I now do according to your word. Behold, I give you a wise and discerning mind … I give you also what you have not asked , both riches and honor" (1 Kings 3:5-14).

We're in the purgative stage.

"He must increase, but I must decrease."
John 3:30

Last year we went from King David to King Solomon.

The apple didn't fall far from the tree.

The End of King Solomon

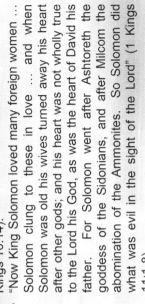

- "Now the weight of gold that came to Solomon in one year was six hundred sixty-six talents" (1 Kings 10:14).
- "Now King Solomon loved many foreign women … Solomon clung to these in love … and when Solomon was old his wives turned away his heart after other gods; and his heart was not wholly true to the Lord his God, as was the heart of David his father. For Solomon went after Ashtoreth the goddess of the Sidonians, and after Milcom the abomination of the Ammonites. So Solomon did what was evil in the sight of the Lord" (1 Kings 11:1-8).

The Loss of the First Love

"I have acquired great wisdom, surpassing all who were over Jerusalem before me … I perceived that this also is but a striving after wind … I searched with my mind how to cheer my body with wine … I made great works … whatever my eyes desired I did not keep from them; I kept my heart from no pleasure … and behold all was vanity and a striving after wind … so I hated life … and gave my heart up to despair." Ecclesiastes 1:16 – 2:20).

(Slide 1)

King Solomon had his heart set on money, but it wasn't just his heart.

Men have some challenges in their brains when it comes to money and success.

Competing Brain Systems

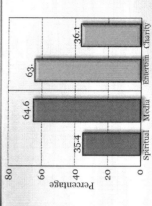

1. Success System:
   - Testosterone increases when we compete.
   - Reward circuitry activated by success – dumping of dopamine.
2. Generosity System:
   - Reward circuitry activated by compassion and generosity.
   - Happiness increases with generosity.
   - Money is a tool to be used for others!
3. Purchases System:
   - Reward circuitry of brain activated by thought to purchase desirable product.
   - Pain circuitry activated by thought of paying.
   - Credit helps to separate pleasure/pain circuitry.

Source: Bollman, S., "The Choice Wine: Seven Steps to a Superabundant Marriage," Chapter 3, The GreenLeaf Group, 2015.)

Competing Brain Systems

- "The harmony in which [Adam and Eve] had found themselves … is now destroyed" (Catechism #400).
- "The eye of the covetous man is insatiable … he will not be satisfied till he consume his own soul" (Sirach 14:9).
- Success System:
  - Brain builds tolerance to dopamine, requiring greater levels of success to achieve same level of satisfaction.
  - Forty percent of individuals with net wealth above $5M do NOT consider themselves wealthy.
- Generosity System:
  - Pain at thought of giving away money.
  - Individuals who give money away feel wealthier than those who don't.

Source: Bollman, S., "The Choice Wine: Seven Steps to a Superabundant Marriage," Chapter 3, The GreenLeaf Group, 2015.)

The Reality of Financial Problems

- Approximately ¼ of couples experience financial stress in a given year.
- Spending money foolishly more than doubles the likelihood of divorce.
- Media consumption raises desires for material goods.
- Approximately two-thirds of TMIY men spend more time on the media than their spiritual lives and spend more money on entertainment than give to charity.

Source: NPR, Robert Wood Johnson Foundation/Harvard School of Public Health, "The Burden of Stress in America," 2014.
"A Longitudinal Study of Marital Problems and Subsequent Divorce," Journal of Marriage and Family, 1997.
"The Influence of Media Exposure on Materialism, Fashion Innovativeness and Cognitive Age: A Multi-Country Study," Proceedings of the 2008 Academy of Marketing Science Annual Conference.
TMIY Internal Data.

Recovering your First Love

- Money is a resource entrusted to you to be placed at the service of other people.
- Think back to the first time you held your first child.
- In your heart, you promised that child you would do anything for him or her. You would give him or her your money, but above all you would give your time and your love.
- Those desires were beautiful.
- Unfortunately, life gets in the way.
- Perhaps we should work to recover our first love.

Man has disharmony within himself.

He must detach from worldly success and the material goods attained by success.

He must learn to use the goods of this world for the betterment of his fellow man.

Taming the Triple Concupiscence

- "All that is in the world, the concupiscence of the flesh and the concupiscence of the eyes and the pride of life, is not of the Father" (1 John 2:16).
- Concupiscence of the flesh: penance and mortification.
- Concupiscence of the eyes: charity.
- Pride of life: prayer.

The Demands of Charity

- "Respect for human dignity requires the practice of the virtue of temperance, so as to moderate attachment to this world's goods" (Catechism #2407).
- "The precept of detachment from riches is obligatory for entrance into the Kingdom of heaven" (Catechism #2544).
- Live below your means.
- Be generous with your financial resources.
- Be generous in your praise of others.

Building a Spiritual Plan of Life

1. Develop Intentionality
   - Entrust your finances to St. Joseph.
   - Begin tithing to the Church.
   - Make it tangible: physically write a check or take money out of your wallet.

2. Get the Grace Flowing
   - Attend Mass more frequently – especially Wed, which is dedicated to St. Joseph.
   - Increase Prayer – in general, when making decisions, novena to St. Joseph.

TMIY
THAT MAN IS YOU!
BECOMING A MAN AFTER GOD'S OWN HEART

Building a Spiritual Plan of Life

3. Form your Mind Correctly
   - Turn off media.
   - Read teachings of the Church (Catechism, Rerum Novarum, Compendium of Social Doctrine."

4. Change Behavior
   - Get out of all debt.
   - Reduce consumption – especially media and entertainment expenses.
   - Make a budget.
   - Become generous with family and those God places in your path.

TMIY
THAT MAN IS YOU!
BECOMING A MAN AFTER GOD'S OWN HEART

Building a Spiritual Plan of Life

5. Establishing Support and Friendships
   - End friendships that lead you to spend money frivolously beyond your means.
   - Avoid people with an overly worldly attitude.
   - Consider taking a course on finances such as "Financial Peace University" by Dave Ramsey.

TMIY
THAT MAN IS YOU!
BECOMING A MAN AFTER GOD'S OWN HEART

Developing the Spirit of Nazareth

1. The Way of Love
   - Do not place professional desires above good of family.
   - Consider money as a tool for the betterment of your family.
   - Consciously endeavor to leave an inheritance to your "children's children."

2. Decreasing Selfishness
   - Place own needs and desires below those of your family.
   - Talk with your wife before any "large" purchases.
   - Don't spend time/money entertaining apart from family.
   - Eat at home together as a family.

3. Increasing Charity
   - Begin tithing to the Church.
   - Help those in need in your immediate influence.

Finances as a Pathway to God

- "Look at the birds of the air: they neither sow nor reap nor gather into barns, and yet your heavenly Father feeds them … Consider the lilies of the field, how they grow; they neither toil nor spin … your heavenly Father knows that you need them all. But seek first his kingdom and his righteousness, and all these things shall be yours as well" (Matthew 6:26-33).
- "A good man leaves an inheritance to his children's children" (Proverbs 13:22).

Evaluation on Use Money for Others

1. Have I stolen anything – including expense report and income taxes?
2. Have I been dishonest in a business transaction?
3. Do I spend money in a way that causes tension with my spouse?
4. Do I spend more time on the media than my spiritual life?
5. Do my conversations typically revolve around business, sports or news?
6. Do I spend more money on all forms of entertainment combined than I give to charity?
7. Do I have credit card debt that I do not pay off each month?
8. Do I give 10% of my income to the Church?
9. Do I save money to leave as an inheritance for my children?
10. Do I give money to help those in need?

Finances are called to called to develop communion between man and God and between peoples.

They are not called to foster selfishness.

I would suggest a 10 question evaluation.

Small Group Discussion

Starter Questions

1. How much tension do you have in your life related to money?
2. What is the single step you are willing to take today to help with your finances?

Next Week

Give God some of your Time

Slide 1

We wish to "increase in wisdom and in stature and in favor with God and man."

(Luke 2:52)

We need to follow Christ in his journey to Nazareth.

Slide 2

Developing the Spirit of Nazareth

1. 7 Steps: Give God some of your time.
2. Character: King Henry VIII.
3. Spiritual Issue: Pride/competing brain systems.
4. State of TMIY men: Best covenant.
5. Spiritual Remedy: Time in Prayer
6. Path to Success: Encounter Christ.
7. Suggested Examine: 10 questions on prayer life.

Slide 3

SESSION 6

Give God Some of your Time

TMIY
THAT MAN IS YOU!
BECOMING A MAN AFTER GOD'S OWN HEART

Slide 4

Nazareth and the Spiritual Life

7 Steps of That Man is You!

1. Honor your wedding vows.
2. Use money for others.
3. Give God some of your time.
4. Set your mind on the things above.
5. Find God in yourself.
6. Find God in other people.
7. Make it easy to be good and hard to be bad.

3 Stages of the Spiritual Life

1. Give away your body.
2. Give away your goods.
3. Give away your time.   } Purgative Stage
4. Receiving illumination from God.   } Illuminative Stage
5. Union with God in self.
6. Union with God through others.   } Unitive Stage
7. Ultimate union with God.

King Henry VIII

- 1485: Henry VII usurps throne of England.
- 1491: Henry VIII is born.
- 1509: Marries Catherine of Aragon; Crowned King of England.
- 1533: Marries Anne Boleyn
- 1534: Declared Head of Church in England.
- 1536: Executes Anne Boleyn
- 1536-1547: Marries 4 additional wives.
- 1547: Dies on January 8th.

King Henry VIII: A Bad End

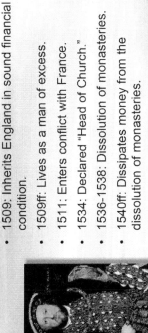

- 1509: Inherits England in sound financial condition.
- 1509ff: Lives as a man of excess.
- 1511: Enters conflict with France.
- 1534: Declared "Head of Church."
- 1536-1538: Dissolution of monasteries.
- 1540ff: Dissipates money from the dissolution of monasteries.
- 1544: Borrows money to invade France.
- 1547: Dies without succession plan – political chaos and civil war.

We're still in the purgative stage.

"He must increase, but I must decrease."
John 3:30

King Henry VIII certainly needed to decrease.

Head of the Church in England

- "For the increase of virtue in Christ's religion within this realm of England, and to repress and extirpate all errors, heresies, and other enormities and abuses heretofore used in the same, be it enacted, by authority of this present Parliament, that the king, our sovereign lord … shall be taken, accepted, and reputed the only supreme head in earth of the Church of England."

- "Any person … do maliciously wish, will or desire … to deprive [royal family] of any of their dignity, title or name … by express writing or words, that the king should be heretic, schismatic, tyrant, infidel or usurper of the crown … shall be reputed, accepted , and adjudged high treason."

Source: "The Act of Supremacy" (1534).
http://www.britainexpress.com/History/tudor/supremacy-henry-text.htm.
Treasons Act 1534,
http://nv18.americau.edu/~diagel/1534treasons.htm.

Competing Brain Systems

1. "I'm in Charge" System:
   - Dorsal Premammillary Nucleus (inside the hypothalamus).
   - Instinctive "one-upmanship" area.
   - Defends territory and status.
2. Prayer System:
   - Anterior cingulate: prayer increases activity leading to great empathy and compassion.
   - Hypothalamus: prayer reduces activity in the "one-upmanship" area of the brain.
   - Caudate Nucleus: prayer increases activity in the reward circuitry of the brain.

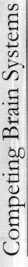

Source: according to [...] the best brain. Penguin Books, New York, 2010, p. xv
Newberg, A, et al., "How God Changes Your Brain," Ballantine Books, New York, 2010, pp. 43-55.
Schjoelt, U, et al., "Rewarding Prayers," Neuroscience Letters 443 (2008) pp. 165-168.

Henry VIII had a big problem with the "pride of life."

We are called to recognize God's sovereignty over us.

You must help your brain make a choice.

The Time We Give to God

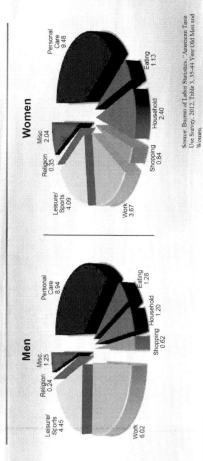

Men

Religion 0.24
Misc. 1.25
Personal Care 8.94
Eating 1.28
Household 1.20
Shopping 0.62
Work 6.02
Leisure/Sports 4.45

Women

Religion 0.35
Misc. 2.04
Personal Care 9.48
Eating 1.13
Household 2.40
Shopping 0.84
Work 3.67
Leisure/Sports 4.09

Source: Bureau of Labor Statistics, "American Time Use Survey, 2012, Table 3, 35-44 Year Old Men and Women.

The Fundamental Choice

- "How are you fallen from heaven … You said in your heart, 'I will ascend to heaven; above the stars of God I will set my throne on high … I will ascend above the heights of the clouds, I will make myself like the Most High" (Isaiah 14:12-14).

- "I am the vine, you are the branches. He who abides in me, and I in him, he it is that bears much fruit, for apart from me you can do nothing. If a man does not abide in me, he is cast forth as a branch and withers" (John 15:5-6).

The Spiritual Life of TMIY Men

- Mass: Three of four every Sunday. Almost half more than weekly.
- Confession: Almost two of three annual. One quarter monthly.
- Morning and Night Prayer: 42%
- Actively avoid commitments to work on spiritual life: about one-third.
- Nightly Examine: one in five.
- Spiritual Plan of Life: one in five.

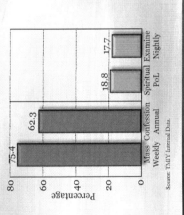

Bar chart — Percentage:
- Mass Weekly: 75.4
- Confession Annual: 62.3
- Spiritual PoL: 18.8
- Examine Nightly: 17.7

Source: TMIY Internal Data

The starting point in the spiritual life is an encounter with Jesus Christ.

He helps us to rediscover our first love.

The story of the Samaritan woman at the well.

Rediscovering the First Love

"Jesus, wearied as he was with the journey, sat down beside the well. It was about the sixth hour [noon]. There came a woman of Samaria to draw water. Jesus said to her, 'Give me a drink' ... The Samaritan woman said to him, 'How is it that you, a Jew, ask a drink of me, a woman of Samaria?' ... Jesus answered her, 'If you knew the gift of God, and who it is that is saying to you, "Give me a drink," you would have asked him and he would have given you living water.' The woman said to him, 'Sir, you have nothing to draw with, and the well is deep.'

John 4:4-12

Rediscovering the First Love

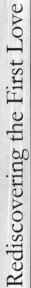

"Jesus said to her, 'Every one who drinks of this water will thirst again, but whoever drinks of the water that I shall give him will never thirst; the water that I shall give him will become in him a spring of water welling up to eternal life.' The woman said to him, 'Sir, give me this water, that I may not thirst, nor come here again.' Jesus said to her, 'Go, call your husband and come here.' The woman answered him, 'I have no husband.' Jesus said to her '... you have had five husbands, and he whom you now have is not your husband' ... "

John 4:13-18

Building a Spiritual Plan of Life

TMIY — THAT MAN IS YOU!
BECOMING A MAN AFTER GOD'S OWN HEART

1. Daily
   - Consecrate the day to God or Our Lady.
   - Morning and Evening Prayer (e.g. Scripture, Rosary, Divine Office)
   - Brief Examination of Conscience.
2. Weekly
   - Mass on Sunday – break from work.
   - Spiritual devotion (e.g. Eucharistic Adoration or talk.

Rediscovering the First Love

TMIY — THAT MAN IS YOU!
BECOMING A MAN AFTER GOD'S OWN HEART

"The woman said to him, 'Sir, I perceive that you are a prophet. Our fathers worshiped on this mountain; and you say that in Jerusalem is the place where men ought to worship.' Jesus said to her, 'Woman, believe me, the hour is coming when neither on this mountain nor in Jerusalem will you worship the Father … But the hour is coming, and now is, when the true worshippers will worship the Father in spirit and in truth, for such the Father seeks to worship him.'"

John 4:19-23

Developing the Spirit of Nazareth

1. The Way of Love
   - Give time to God in your family members.
   - Pray with and for your family members.
   - Enjoy time together with family as entertainment.
2. Ecclesia Domestica
   - "My house shall be called a house of prayer" (Matthew 21:13).
   - Pray with and for your family members.
   - Make a sacrifice for the needs of your family members.
3. Union with Church
   - Bring the Liturgical life of the Church into your home.
   - Celebrate Advent/Christmas and Lent/Easter in special way.
   - Establish "family feast days" for favorite saints.

Building a Spiritual Plan of Life

3. Monthly
   - Special Feast Day or Devotion (e.g. First Friday to Sacred Heart or Feast Days of Our Lady).
   - Confession
4. Annual
   - Review Spiritual Plan of Life.
   - Make a retreat.
   - Pray a Novena.
5. Life Time
   - Pilgrimage

Evaluation on Prayer Life

1. Do I go to Mass every Sunday?
2. Do I go to Confession at least once per year?
3. Do I begin and end each day in prayer?
4. Do I take time to pray during the course of the day?
5. Does my prayer life include moments of silence so that I can listen to God?
6. Do I do a brief examination of conscience at the end of every day?
7. Do I pray with my spouse and/or children?
8. Do I celebrate Feast Days of the Church in addition to Christmas and Easter?
9. Do I have a Spiritual Plan of Life?
10. Do I avoid other commitments to fulfill my spiritual activities and Plan of Life?

Your prayer life is called to be the foundation for your spiritual life.

It should be rigorous and robust.

I would suggest a 10 question evaluation.

Small Group Discussion

Starter Questions

1. Are you willing to develop a Spiritual Plan of Life? Will you do it by Christmas?
2. What is the single action you need to make to take the next step in your prayer life?

Next Week
Set Your Mind on the Things Above

We wish to "increase in wisdom and in stature and in favor with God and man."

(Luke 2:52)

We need to follow Christ in his journey to Nazareth.

SESSION 7

Set your Mind on the Things Above

Developing the Spirit of Nazareth

1. 7 Steps: Set your mind on the things above.
2. Character: Alexis Carrel.
3. Spiritual Issue: Material apparent vs. spiritual.
4. State of TMIY men: Taking first steps.
5. Spiritual Remedy: Embrace Divine Revelation.
6. Path to Success: Intellectual Formation
7. Suggested Examine: 10 questions on formation of the mind.

Nazareth and the Spiritual Life

7 Steps of That Man is You!

1. Honor your wedding vows.
2. Use money for others.
3. Give God some of your time.
4. Set your mind on the things above.
5. Find God in yourself.
6. Find God in other people.
7. Make it easy to be good and hard to be bad.

3 Stages of the Spiritual Life

1. Give away your body.
2. Give away your goods.
3. Give away your time. — Purgative Stage
4. Receiving illumination from God. — Illuminative Stage
5. Union with God in self.
6. Union with God through others.
7. Ultimate union with God. — Unitive Stage

Entry into the Illuminative Way

"If then you have been raised with Christ, seek the things that are above, where Christ is, seated at the right hand of God. Set your minds on the things that are above, not on the things that are on earth. For you have died, and your life is hid with Christ in God."

Colossians 3:1-3

This week, we are called to make a major transition in the spiritual life.

We are called to enter into the illuminative way.

It may not be as easy as you think.

"Gentle Virgin, who bringeth help to the unfortunate who humbly implore thee. Keep me with thee. I believe in thee. Thou didst answer my prayers by a blazing miracle. I am still blind to it. I still doubt. But the greatest desire of my life, my highest aspiration, is to believe, to believe passionately, implicitly, and never more to analyze and doubt. Thy name is more gracious than the morning sun. Take unto thyself this uneasy sinner with the anxious frown and troubled heart who has exhausted himself in the vain pursuit of fantasies. Beneath the deep, harsh warnings of my intellectual pride a smothered dream persists. Alas, it is still only a dream, but the most enchanting of them all. It is the dream of believing in thee and of loving thee with the shining spirit of the men of God."

The Story of Alexis Carrel

- 1873: Born to devout parents in Lyon, France.
- 1900: Doctor of Medicine, Lyon University.
- 1889-1900: Becomes a practical atheist while pursuing academic degrees.
- 1902: Publishes work on suture of blood vessels.
- 1912: Awarded Nobel Prize in Medicine.
- 1902: During trip to Lourdes, witnesses instantaneous cure of Marie Bailly at the point of death from tubercular peritonitis.

The Story of Alexis Carrel

- 1910: Witnesses 2nd instantaneous cure of a 18 month old child born blind. Marries nurse.
- Struggles to accept faith until end of life.
- 1938: Meets Dom Alexis Presse.
- 1942: "I believe in the existence of God, in the immortality of the soul, in Revelation and in all that the Catholic Church teaches."
- "When one approaches one's own death, one grasps the nothingness of all things. I have gained fame. The world speaks of me and of my works, yet I am a mere child before God, and a poor child at that."
- 1945: Dies on November 5th.

The biggest issue with our intellect is we continue to allow it to be less than it was created to be.

We stop at the external and superficial instead of going to the depths.

The Temptation to Lessen the Mind

- "You were within me and I was outside, and there I sought for you and in my ugliness I plunged into the beauties that you have made. You were with me, and I was not with you" (Confessions, Book X, Chapter 27).
- "[Men] by their wickedness suppress the truth. For what can be known about God is plain to them, because God has shown it to them. Ever since the creation of the world his invisible nature … has been clearly perceived … in the things that have been made. So they are without excuse … they became futile in their thinking and their senseless minds were darkened" (Romans 1:18-21).

The Potential of the Human Mind

1. Natural Knowledge
   - The ability of the mind to know God unaided by divine revelation.
   - Properly speaking: metaphysics.
   - Today physical sciences are a launching point.
2. Divine Revelation
   - The ability of the mind to know God through divine revelation.
3. Contemplative or Mystical
   - The ability of the mind to know God through contemplative or mystical union with God.

The Challenge for Modern Man

The first swallow from the cup of natural sciences makes atheists, but at the bottom of the cup God is waiting.

Werner Heisenberg
Nobel Laureate, Physics, 1932

Jesus Christ is the "light of the world."
(John 8:12)

We must allow his light to envelop our minds.

The Potential of the Human Mind

- Intellectual pursuits are granted their appropriate autonomy.
- They should be guided my moral principles and divine truth.
- Evolution: "The Teaching Authority of the Church does not forbid ... research and discussions ... with regard to the doctrine of evolution ... the Catholic faith obliges us to hold that souls are immediately created by God" (Pope Pius XII, Humani Generis, #36).
- The Choice Wine – Chapter 5.

The Gift of Divine Revelation

- "Sacred tradition, Sacred Scripture and the teaching authority of the Church ... are so linked and joined together that one cannot stand without the others" (Dei Verbum, #10).
- Scripture: "You search the scriptures, because you think that in them you have eternal life; and it is they that bear witness to me" (John 5:39).
- Tradition: "Stand firm and hold to the traditions which you were taught by us, either by word of mouth or by letter" (2 Thessalonians 2:15).
- Magisterium: "He who hears you hears me" (Luke 10:16).

TMIY Men and Intellectual Formation

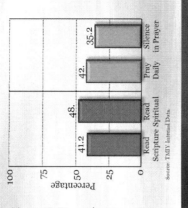

Percentage

- Read Scripture: 41.2
- Read Spiritual: 48.
- Pray Daily: 42.
- Silence in Prayer: 35.2

Source: TMIY Internal Data.

- Scripture: Approximately 40 percent read Scripture on a *regular* basis.
- Spiritual Books: Almost half read spiritual books or watch spiritual programming on a regular basis.
- Morning and Night Prayer: Just over 42 percent begin and end day in prayer.
- Silence: Approximately one-third include silence in their prayer.

The Pursuit of Wisdom

- "Contemplative prayer in my opinion is nothing else than a close sharing between friends; it means taking time frequently to be alone with him who we know loves us" (St. Teresa of Avila, Catechism, #2709).
- "Contemplative prayer is a union with the prayer of Christ insofar as it makes us participate in this mystery" (Catechism #2718).
- "Contemplative prayer is silence, the 'symbol of the world to come' or 'silent love'" (Catechism #2717).

Building a Spiritual Plan of Life

TMIY
THAT MAN IS YOUR
BECOMING A MAN AFTER GOD'S OWN HEART

1. Substantially reduce media consumption.
   - Avoid all content contrary to the faith or morals of the Church.
   - Reduce morally neutral content since it takes time from spiritual pursuits.
2. Read Scripture practicing Lectio Divina
   - Spend 15 minutes a day reading Scripture.
   - Reading, Meditation, Prayer, Contemplation.

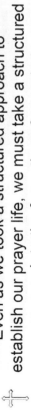

Even as we took a structured approach to establish our prayer life, we must take a structured approach to the formation of our mind.

Developing the Spirit of Nazareth

1. The Way of Love
   - Created to God's "image and likeness" (Genesis 1:26), the human person is the crowning point of creation.
   - Truly discover the miracle of life.
2. Nature
   - Enjoy nature with your family as a means to encounter God.
   - Go on pilgrimage – God will speak to you.
3. Scripture
   - Create a home free of endless, mindless noise and clutter.
   - Discuss Sunday readings and homily.
   - Read Scripture together with your family.
   - Read Scripture frequently enough that it becomes a normal reference point in conversations.

Small Group Discussion

Starter Questions

1. How are you going to get the media under control in your personal life?
2. Will you read Scripture at least once per week? With another person? Who?

Next Week
Find God in Yourself

Building a Spiritual Plan of Life

3. Read spiritual works on a regular basis.
   - Read Magisterial documents – writings of the Pope (especially an encyclical).
   - Read writings from the saints.
4. Enjoy Beauty
   - Enjoy nature – say Rosary in nature.
   - Enjoy the arts or a beautiful church.
5. Pray
   - Build a rigorous prayer life.
   - Include time of silence in God's presence.

Evaluation on Elevating the Mind to God

1. Do I consume media with content contrary to the faith and morals of the Church?
2. Do I spend more time on the media than my spiritual life?
3. Do I participate in conversations that are contrary to the faith and morals of the Church?
4. Do I have friendships with people who are against the Church or are totally focused on worldly pursuits?
5. Do I take time to enjoy the beauty of nature and/or the arts?
6. Do I read Scripture every day?
7. Have I read or studied the Catechism to learn our faith?
8. Do I read new documents by the Pope?
9. Do I read the writings and lives of the saints?
10. Does my prayer include silence to listen to God?

Slide 1 (top left)

We wish to "increase in wisdom and in stature and in favor with God and man."

(Luke 2:52)

We need to follow Christ in his journey to Nazareth.

Slide 2 (top right)

Developing the Spirit of Nazareth

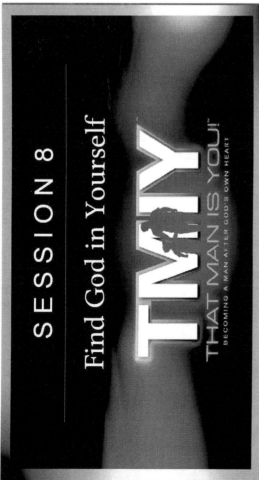

1. 7 Steps: Find God in Yourself.
2. Character: John Pridmore.
3. Spiritual Issue: Human limitations and failings.
4. State of TMIY men: Taking first steps.
5. Spiritual Remedy: Eucharist.
6. Path to Success: Become "rich in mercy."
7. Suggested Examine: 10 questions on moral life and merciful disposition.

Slide 3 (bottom left)

SESSION 8

Find God in Yourself

Slide 4 (bottom right)

Nazareth and the Spiritual Life

7 Steps of That Man is You!

1. Honor your wedding vows.
2. Use money for others.
3. Give God some of your time.
4. Set your mind on the things above.
5. Find God in yourself.
6. Find God in other people.
7. Make it easy to be good and hard to be bad.

3 Stages of the Spiritual Life

1. Give away your body.
2. Give away your goods.
3. Give away your time.
4. Receiving illumination from God.
5. Union with God in self.
6. Union with God through others.
7. Ultimate union with God.

Purgative Stage

Illuminative Stage

Unitive Stage

Entry into the Unitive Way

"If a man loves me, he will keep my word, and my Father will love him, and we will come to him and make our home with him."

John 14:23

This week, we make another major transition in the spiritual life.

We are called to enter into the unitive way.

We are fortunate that God is merciful.

The Descent of John Pridmore

- When his parents get a divorce, they ask John to choose which one he wants to live with.
- He can't choose. He loves them both.
- He unconsciously decides to never love again. It's too painful.
- By mid 20's, he lives a life of rage.
- He's going to collect a debt with instructions to hurt someone very badly if he doesn't pay.
- Meets a young boy on a lift: "Jesus loves you."
- "I'm glad someone does."

Source: Pridmore, J., "Gangland to Promised Land – One Man's Journey from the Criminal Underworld to Christ," Lighthouse Catholic Media, Sycamore, IL, 2011.

The Story of John Pridmore

- Born in 1964 in London.
- Age 11: After his parents divorce, made the unconscious decision to no longer love.
- Age 14: Started stealing.
- Age 15: Placed in a youth detention center.
- Age 19: Placed in an adult prison.
- Age 20: Entered London's underworld, working as an enforcer in the mafia and dealing drugs.
- Age 27: Left a man for dead outside a pub.
- Age 44: Spoke to 400,000 youth at World Youth Day in Sydney, Australia.

Source: Pridmore, J., "Gangland to Promised Land – One Man's Journey from the Criminal Underworld to Christ," Lighthouse Catholic Media, Sycamore, IL, 2011.

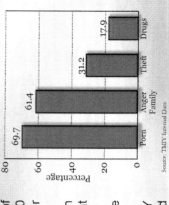

TMIY Men and the Moral Life

- Sex: Approximately 70 percent of TMIY men view pornography; 30 percent have cheated on their spouse.
- Anger: Over 60 percent of TMIY men have raised their voice in anger at their wife and children.
- Theft: One-third of TMIY men have stolen something.
- Drugs: Just under one-fifth of TMIY men have used illicit drugs or abused prescription drugs.

Source: TMIY Internal Data.

There's good news!

You guys are in much better shape than the average mafia enforcer!

If he attained reconciliation with God, so can you.

Two Competing Realities

- The four living creatures ... day and night they never cease to sing, 'Holy, holy, holy, is the Lord God Almighty, who was and is and is to come'" (Revelation 4:8).
- "Nothing unclean shall enter it, nor any one who practices abomination or falsehood" (Revelation 21:27).
- "All have sinned and fall short of the glory of God" (Romans 3:23).

The Conversion of John Pridmore

- Leaves a man for dead outside a London pub and is hiding from police.
- Mother: "I've prayed for you every day of your life. But two weeks ago ... I prayed to Jesus to take you. If it meant you dying, then to let you die, but not to let you hurt yourself or anyone else any more."
- Hears a voice telling him every sin he has done.
- Feels as if he is sinking into hell.
- Cries out: "Give me one more chance."
- Opens Bible and reads the story of the Prodigal Son. Breaks down crying and is converted.

Source: Pridmore, J., "Gangland to Promised Land – One Man's Journey from the Criminal Underworld to Christ," Lighthouse Catholic Media, Sycamore, IL, 2011.

The Eucharistic Miracle of Lanciano

- 8th Century Lanciano, Italy
- Priest – doubting the Real Presence – had just said the words of consecration.
- Host turned into Flesh and Wine turned into Blood.
- Sacred Species maintained ever since.
- Scientific experiments in 1971 and 1981.
- Flesh is human flesh from the heart.
- Blood is human blood. Proteins in blood are from "fresh" human blood.
- Blood type for both is AB.
- Blood type matches that of the Shroud of Turin.

Source: Real Presence Eucharistic Education and Adoration Association, Inc., "The Eucharistic Miracles of the World," Eternal Life, KY, 2009 pp. 122-125. Cruz, J., "Eucharistic Miracles," Tan Books and Publishers, IL, 1987, pp. 3-18.

Even in our fallen state, we can all hope for union with God. Indeed, he gave us the perfect means.

"He who eats my flesh and drinks my blood abides in me, and I in him."

(John 6:56)

God dwells within you! He wants to live his divine life in and through you.

It is the life of Father.

It is the life of the Divine Bridegroom.

The Practice of the Presence of God

"I cannot express to you what is taking place in me at present … I devote myself exclusively to remaining always in his holy presence. I keep myself in his presence by simple attentiveness and a general loving awareness of God that I call 'actual presence of God' or better, a quiet and secret conversation of the soul with God that is lasting."

Brother Lawrence

The Life of the Divine Bridegroom

- Jesus is the divine bridegroom.
- "Husbands, love your wives, as Christ loved the Church and gave himself up for her, that he might sanctify her … that he might present the church to himself in splendor, without spot or wrinkle or any such thing, that she might be holy and without blemish" (Ephesians 5:25-27).
- We are called to offer ourselves in sacrifice for the purity of our spouses in small ways throughout the day.
- We are called to make sacrifice when she is "least worthy."

The Life of Father

"Men relive and reveal on earth the very fatherhood of God" (Cf. St. John Paul II, Familiaris Consortio, #25).

1. Source of Life
   - "As the Father has life in himself, so he has granted the Son also to have life in himself" (John 5:25).
2. Holiness – evil remains on outside the home:
   - "Nothing unclean shall enter it, nor any one who practices abomination or falsehood" (Revelation 21:27).
3. Superabundant Joy:
   - "He will wipe away every tear from their eyes … neither shall there be mourning nor crying nor pain any more" (Revelation 21:4).

Building a Spiritual Plan of Life

1. Substantially reduce media consumption.
   - Avoid all content contrary to the faith or morals of the Church.
   - Reduce morally neutral content since it takes time from spiritual pursuits.
2. Live the moral life more profoundly.
   - Embrace ascetical practices as necessary.
   - Avoid all serious sin.
   - Go to confession once per month.
3. Live a more profound Eucharistic life.
   - Receive the Eucharist as frequently as possible.
   - Practice the Presence of God.

TMIY
THAT MAN IS YOU!
BECOMING A MAN AFTER GOD'S OWN HEART

We are called to find God dwelling within ourselves.

It will relate to the life we live.

There are five major steps.

Building a Spiritual Plan of Life

TMIY
"THAT MAN IS YOU!"
BECOMING A MAN AFTER GOD'S OWN HEART

4. Encounter God the Father in your fatherhood
   - Be a source of life for your family, which includes providing for them.
   - Battle evil – keep it out of your heart and home.
   - Fill your home with joy – have fun!
   - Be "rich in mercy" (Cf. Ephesians 2:4).
5. Live the life of the Divine Bridegroom
   - Love your wife enough to lay down your life for her.
   - Live a sacrificial life in small things every day.
   - Be willing to make a sacrifice for her whenever she is "least worthy."

Developing the Spirit of Nazareth

1. The Way of Love
   - Develop a preferential desire to be with your family.
   - Make sure professional/social activities are in harmony with your desire to be present to your family.
   - Have a sacrificial disposition in small things every day.
2. Battling Evil
   - Work to keep all evil outside your heart and home.
   - When there is tension be the first to seek reconciliation.
3. Finding Superabundant Joy
   - Have fun with your family as your preferred entertainment.
   - "Let your children run, jump and make as much noise as they like, so long as they don't sin" (St. John Bosco).

Evaluation on Finding God in Self

1. Do I consume media with content contrary to the faith and morals of the Church?
2. Do I use illicit drugs or misuse prescription drugs?
3. Do I drink alcohol in a way that causes problems for me or my family?
4. Do I respect the body by getting sufficient sleep, eating a healthy diet and regular exercise?
5. Have I had a vasectomy or my wife a tubal ligation?
6. Do I actively seek to keep evil outside my home – beginning with my own electronic equipment?
7. Do I receive the Eucharist more frequently than Sunday?
8. Do I sacrifice my own pursuits to spend more time with my wife and children?
9. Do I make a sacrifice for the purity of my wife at least weekly?
10. Do I explicitly help my wife and children live a more devout Christian life?

Small Group Discussion

Starter Questions

1. Where do you need to remove evil from your heart and from your home?
2. What sacrifice do you need to make to be a better husband and father?

Next Week
Find God in Other People

We wish to "increase in wisdom and in stature and in favor with God and man."
(Luke 2:52)

We need to follow Christ in his journey to Nazareth.

Developing the Spirit of Nazareth

THAT MAN IS YOU!
BECOMING A MAN AFTER GOD'S OWN HEART

1. 7 Steps: Find God in Other People.
2. Character: Eminem
3. Spiritual Issue: Failings of other people.
4. State of TMIY men: Working on it.
5. Spiritual Remedy: Mercy and kindness.
6. Path to Success: The dignity of the person.
7. Suggested Examine: 10 questions on spiritual nature of friendships.

SESSION 9

Find God in Other People

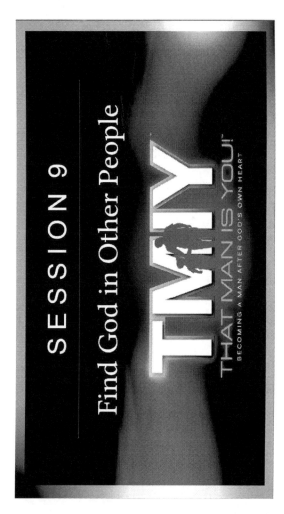

TMIY
THAT MAN IS YOU!
BECOMING A MAN AFTER GOD'S OWN HEART

Nazareth and the Spiritual Life

7 Steps of That Man is You!	3 Stages of the Spiritual Life	
1. Honor your wedding vows.	1. Give away your body.	Purgative Stage
2. Use money for others.	2. Give away your goods.	
3. Give God some of your time.	3. Give away your time.	
4. Set your mind on the things above.	4. Receiving illumination from God.	Illuminative Stage
5. Find God in yourself.	5. Union with God in self.	Unitive Stage
6. Find God in other people.	6. Union with God through others.	
7. Make it easy to be good and hard to be bad.	7. Ultimate union with God.	

Eminem

- Born Marshall Bruce Mathers III in 1972.
- Sold over 155 million albums – best selling artist of the 2000s.
- Approx. 3.5 BILLION views on vevo channel.
- Won Academy Award for Best Song.
- Won 15 Grammy Awards including 6 for Best Rap Album.
- Married/Divorce childhood sweetheart twice.
- Has one daughter – Halley Mathers.
- Took a several year hiatus associated with drug rehab in 2005; resumed in 2009 continued commercial success after 2009.

One of the most powerful sessions in TMIY was on Eminem.

We're going to take another look at him this year.

It hits in a totally different way.

Eminem: Cleanin' Out My Closet

Ha! I got some skeletons in my closet … I'll take you back to '73.
I was a baby, maybe I was just a couple of months
My faggot father must have had his panties up in a bunch
Cause he split, I wonder if he even kissed me goodbye
On second thought I just ****ing wished he would die
I look at Hailie, and I could picture leaving her side
Even if I hated Kim, I'd grit my teeth and I'd try.
To make it work with her at least for Hailie's sake
What I did was stupid, no doubt it was dumb,
But the smartest s*** I did was take the bullets outta the gun
It's my life, I'd like to welcome y'all to 'The Eminem Show'

Eminem: Cleanin' our My Closet

Eminem: Cleanin' Out My Closet

But put yourself in my position; just try to envision
Witnessing your momma popping prescription pills in the kitchen
My whole life I was made to believe I was sick when I wasn't
'Til I grew up, now I blew up, it makes you sick to ya stomach.
You're getting older now and it's cold when you're lonely
And Nathan's growing up so quick he's gonna know you're phony
Hailie's getting so big now; you should see her, she's beautiful
But you'll never see her – she won't even be at your funeral
See what hurts me the most is you won't admit you was wrong.
B**** do your song – keep telling yourself that you was a mom.
But how dare you try to take what you didn't help me to get.
You selfish b****, I hope you f****** burn in hell for this s***.

Eminem: Cleanin' Out My Closet

I'm sorry momma!
I never meant to hurt you!
I never meant to make you cry; but tonight
I'm cleaning out my closet.
I'm sorry momma!
I never meant to hurt you!
I never meant to make you cry; but tonight
I'm cleaning out my closet.

Two Competing Realities

- "Where two or three are gathering in my name, there am I in the midst of them" (Matthew 18:20).
- "Whoever receives one such child in my name, receives me" (Matthew 18:5).
- "As you did it to one of the least of these my brethren, you did it to me" (Matthew 25:40).
- "All have sinned and fall short of the glory of God" (Romans 3:23).

Most of us have not dealt with the exact same issues as Eminem, but we all face challenges in finding God in other people.

The Challenge of Technology

- Mobile technology has been adopted faster than any other technology in history.
- Almost ¾ of parents use their mobile technology while eating out with their children.
- Approximately 70 percent of 6-10 year-olds bring technology to the table.
- Approximately 90 percent of people consider it rude when the person they are with talks to someone else on the telephone.

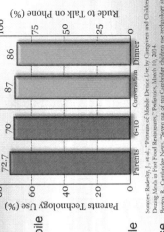

Sources: Radesky, J., et al., "Patterns of Mobile Device Use by Caregivers and Children During Meals in Fast Food Restaurants." Pediatrics, March 10, 2014.
Brown, R. Cambridge News, "Seven out of ten Cambridge children use technology at the dinner table but want to spend more time with parents, study finds," May 28, 2014.
Weber Shandwick, et al., "Civility in America, 2013."

TMIY Men and God in Other People

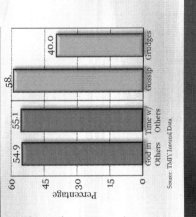

Source: TMIY Internal Data

- Over half of TMIY men discover God's guidance in their lives through another person.
- Over half of TMIY men prefer spending time with others vs. alone.
- Almost 60 percent of TMIY men gossip about others.
- Approximately 40 percent of TMIY hold grudges against another person.

Building a Spiritual Plan of Life

1. Pray for the grace to find God in every person.
2. Treat every person as if he were Jesus Christ – especially the poor and those in need.
   - Treat every person with dignity and respect.
   - Do not always insist on your own opinion or way of doing things.
   - "If any one makes no mistakes in what he says, he is a perfect man" (James 3:2).
3. Evaluate relationships from a spiritual perspective.
   - End friendships that objectively lead you away from God.
   - Seek friendships that lead you to God.

We are called to find God dwelling within other people.

The spiritual reality is not changed just because they are imperfect.

There are five major steps.

Developing the Spirit of Nazareth

1. The Way of Love
   - Have a preferential option to spend time with your family members – especially versus media and technology.
   - Be present to your family members – silence technology, don't text, etc.
   - Speak charitably and never in anger.
   - Listen – don't interrupt; don't insist on your opinion.
2. Pray for Humility to Encounter God
   - Pray for God to speak to you and encounter you through others: "Speak Lord for your servant is listening" (1 Samuel 3:10).
   - Consult your wife on all major decisions.
   - Accept someone as your spiritual mentor or guide.

Building a Spiritual Plan of Life

4. Find God in your children.
   - Give time to your children – it is time given to God.
     - Treat children with dignity and respect.
     - Pray with your children.
     - Help children develop a plan-of-life.
5. Find God in your spouse.
   - Give time to your spouse – it is time given to God.
     - Treat spouse with dignity and respect.
     - Pray with your spouse.
     - Help spouse develop a plan-of-life.

TMIY
THAT MAN IS YOU!
BECOMING A MAN AFTER GOD'S OWN HEART

Small Group Discussion

Starter Questions
1. Who do you need to forgive that has hurt you badly? What are you going to do about it?
2. How are you going to use technology in a way that does not impact your relationships?

Next Week
Make it Easy to be Good and Hard to be Bad

Evaluation on Finding God in Self

1. Do I say "Thank you" and "Please" and listen to others without interrupting?
2. Do I text, email or phone while I am in the presence of others?
3. Do I ask the opinion and help of others?
4. Do I gossip about others?
5. Do I hold grudges against others?
6. Do I raise my voice in anger when speaking with others?
7. Do I have friendships that lead me into sin or inappropriate behavior?
8. Do I have spiritual conversations with my friends on a regular basis?
9. Do I have spiritual conversations with my wife and children on a regular basis?
10. Do I pray with my wife, children and friends on a regular basis?

SESSION 10

Make it Easy to be Good and Hard to be Bad

TMIY
THAT MAN IS YOU!
BECOMING A MAN AFTER GOD'S OWN HEART

We wish to "increase in wisdom and in stature and in favor with God and man."

(Luke 2:52)

We need to follow Christ in his journey to Nazareth.

Developing the Spirit of Nazareth

1. 7 Steps: Make it Easy to be Good and Hard to be Bad
2. Character: Betty Brennan
3. Spiritual Issue: Trust in God's Mercy.
4. State of TMIY men: Working on it.
5. Spiritual Remedy: Confession.
6. Path to Success: Learn mercy – Experience Mercy – "Preventive Mercy"
7. Suggested Examine: 10 questions on mercy.

Nazareth and the Spiritual Life

7 Steps of That Man is You!

1. Honor your wedding vows.
2. Use money for others.
3. Give God some of your time.
4. Set your mind on the things above.
5. Find God in yourself.
6. Find God in other people.
7. Make it easy to be good and hard to be bad.

3 Stages of the Spiritual Life

1. Give away your body.
2. Give away your goods.
3. Give away your time. — Purgative Stage
4. Receiving illumination from God. — Illuminative Stage
5. Union with God in self.
6. Union with God through others. — Unitive Stage
7. Ultimate union with God.

A Powerful Confession

- Fr. Peter called to the bed of a dying man in the hospital.
- Man had been estranged from Church for many years.
- Small talk – eventually man wants to confess.
- Semi-private room – roommate has issues with Church: "That won't do you any good."
- As confession progresses, roommate becomes ever more agitated. Eventually he begins to shout and curse.
- At the words of absolution: "You can't have him, he's ours."
- Roommate is foaming at mouth.

Mercy. We proclaim to believe in the mercy of God.

How far does that mercy extend?

I have two new stories for you.

God's mercy is truly superabundant.

It touched the lives of an atheist, a mafia enforcer and a Satanist .

It can touch your life too – if you trust in God!

The Excess of God's Mercy

- Betty Brennan – raised Catholic; wife and mother; professional musician.
- Two year-old child dies of brain cancer; very angry at God, but cannot express it to anyone.
- Three Satanic priests are in the orchestra. They befriend her. Listen to her anger. Invite her to a Satanic ritual.
- Betty eventually becomes a Satanist and reaches the higher echelons: "I did everything but human sacrifice."
- Begins attending a "healing Mass" with a friend.
- Disrupt services – always leaves before consecration: "Satanists believe more in the sacraments than most Catholics. If you put 2000 hosts in a ciborium and only one was consecrated, I could pick it every time."
- Rushing out of Mass before a consecration and runs directly into a priest: "In the name of Jesus Christ, who are you."
- Begins long process of exorcism and healing.
- Catholic speaker touching the lives of thousands.

Competing Brain Systems

1. Prayer System:
   - Caudate Nucleus: prayer increases activity in the reward circuitry of the brain.
   - Anterior cingulate: prayer increases activity leading to great empathy and compassion.
   - Amygdala: prayer reduces activity in amygdala and limbic system, which reduces fear.
2. Guilt System:
   - Anterior cingulate: shame and guilt increases activity.
   - Amygdala: shame and guilt increase activity, leading to increased fear and anxiety.

Source: Newberg, A. et al., "How God Changes Your Brain," Ballantine Books, New York, 2010, pp. 43-55.
Schjodt, U., et al., "Rewarding Prayers," Neuroscience Letters 443 (2008) pp 165-168.
Michl P., et al., Neurobiological Underpinnings of Shame and Guilt: A Pilot fMRI Study," Social Cognitive and Affective Neuroscience, 2014, 9(2), pp 150-157.

The Fundamental Choice

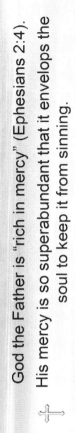

- "Eve took of its fruit and ate, and she also gave some to her husband, and he ate ... the man and his wife hid themselves from the presence of the Lord God among the trees of the garden" (Genesis 3:6-8).
- "As he sat at table ... many tax collectors and sinners came and sat down with Jesus and his disciples ... 'I desire mercy and not sacrifice. For I came not to call the righteous, but sinners'" (Matthew 9:10-13).

TMIY Men and Trust in God

- TMIY men deal with some serious moral issues.
- Approximately two-thirds view pornography and raise their voice at their family members.
- Approximately one-third have cheated on their spouse or visited a topless club.
- Almost two-thirds go to confession at least annually. About one-quarter go to confession monthly.

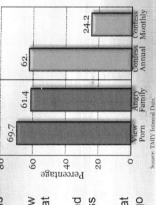

God the Father is "rich in mercy" (Ephesians 2:4).

- His mercy is so superabundant that it envelops the soul to keep it from sinning.

  This is the mercy we seek to receive and share.

Superabundant Mercy in the Home

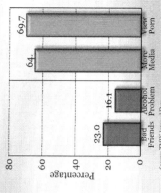

"The preventative system consists in making the laws known and then watching carefully so that the pupils may at all times be under the vigilant eye of the Rector, who like loving fathers can ... place the pupils in the impossibility of committing faults."

Don Bosco

Source: Lemoyne, G., "The Biographical Memoirs of St. John Bosco," v. 4, Salesiana Publishers, Inc., New York, 1967, p. 381.

The Superabundant Mercy of God

- "Through the centuries the Church has become ever more aware that Mary, 'full of grace' through God, was redeemed from the moment of her conception. That is what the dogma of the Immaculate Conception confesses" (Catechism #491).

- "By listening to the woman I shall send to you, you will do everything with ease" (Words of Jesus Christ to Don Bosco).

Source: Lappin, P., "Give Me Souls: Life of Don Bosco," Salesiana Publishers, New York, 1986, "The Lady and the Dream, prior to Chapter 1.

TMIY Men and Problems in Spiritual Life

- Bad Companions: Less than ¼ of TMIY men have friendships that lead them into sin.

- Bad Habits: About 1/6 of TMIY men have issues with alcohol or drugs.

- Bad Books: About two-thirds of TMIY men spend more time on the media than their spiritual life.

- Bad Books: About two-thirds of TMIY men view pornography.

The Road Leading to Hell

"I looked up and read these words: 'The place of no reprieve.' I realized that we were at the gates of hell ... At intervals, many other lads came tumbling down [to hell] after them. I saw one unlucky boy being pushed down the slope by an evil companion. Others fell singly or with others, arm in arm or side by side. Each of them bore the name of his sin on his forehead ... Again the portals would open thunderously and slam shut with a rumble. Then, dead silence! 'Bad companions, bad books and bad habits,' my guide exclaimed, 'are mainly responsible for so many eternally lost.'"

Dream of Don Bosco

Source: Brown, E., "Dreams, Visions and Prophecies of Don Bosco," Don Bosco Publications, New York, 1986, pp. 216-217.

Mercy as the Light to our Path

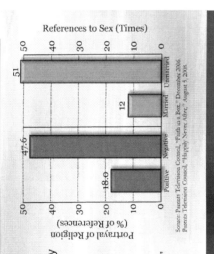

"The light of divine mercy will illumine the way for the men and women of the third millennium ... this consoling message is addressed above all to those who, afflicted by a particularly harsh trial or crushed by the weight of the sins they committed, have lost all confidence in life and are tempted to give in to despair."

Pope John Paul II

Media Depictions of Faith and Family

- The media has become the primary means of education for faith and relationships.
- Formal religious institutions and clearly defined beliefs about God are presented negatively 2.5 times more frequently than positively.
- Marriage is most frequently presented as burdensome and confining.
- Spoken and visual references to unmarried sex outnumber those to married sex 4.25 to 1 in "Family Hour."

Sources: Hjarvard, S., "The Mediatization of Religion," 5th International Conference on Media, Religion, and Culture, Stockholm, 2006

Building a Spiritual Plan of Life

1. Pray to Our Lady and St. Joseph
   - Our Lady and St. Joseph received more mercy than anyone else. They will help you to trust in God's mercy.
2. Increase your trust in Divine Mercy.
   - Hearing the experience other people have of God's mercy helps to believe in his mercy.
   - Read/watch modern conversion stories.
3. Experience the mercy of God.
   - Return to Confession – begin going to Confession on a regular basis (monthly).
   - Encourage family members to make Confession a part of their spiritual life.

TMIY
THAT MAN IS YOUR
BECOMING A MAN AFTER GOD'S OWN HEART

We are called to enter more deeply into the superabundant mercy of God.

There are five major steps.

Developing the Spirit of Nazareth

1. The Way of Love
   - Spend as much time as possible together with your family: "It is not good for man to be alone" (Genesis 2:18).
   - Make the sacraments – especially Communion and Confession – the foundation of your spiritual life.
   - Have a sacrificial disposition for your family members.
2. Superabundant Joy
   - Learn to have fun in your home – God brings communion and joy.
   - "Let your children run, jump and make as much noise as they like, so long as they don't sin" (St. John Bosco).
3. Preventive Mercy
   - Organize your home and personal life so that it is "easy to be good and hard to be bad."

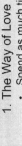

Small Group Discussion

Starter Questions

1. What is the most amazing conversion story you have ever heard?
2. What are 3 actions you can take to make it easy to be good and hard to be bad?

Next Week

Developing a Spiritual Plan of Life

Building a Spiritual Plan of Life

4. Practice Preventive Mercy
   - Avoid people/things that lead to sin.
   - Substantially reduce media consumption and be more discerning.
   - Put in place appropriate filters on all electronic equipment.
   - Establish a "buddy system."
5. Forgive those who have hurt you deeply.
   - Christ died praying for those who crucified him.
   - Forgiving others will free you.

TMIY
THAT MAN IS YOUR
BECOMING A MAN AFTER GOD'S OWN HEART

Evaluation on Experiencing God's Mercy

1. Can I name all of the Ten Commandments?
2. Do I go to Confession at least once per year?
3. Do I go to Confession at least once per month?
4. Do I do a nightly examination of conscience and ask for God's mercy?
5. At home, do I spend more time together with my family than I do alone?
6. Do I take specific actions to help me avoid sin and the occasions of sin?
7. Do I perform an act of penance or mortification at least once per week?
8. Do I perform an act of penance or mortification for my family at least once per week?
9. Do I personally live the moral life I expect my family members to live?
10. Have I forgiven those who have hurt me deeply?

SESSION 11

Developing a Spiritual Plan of Life

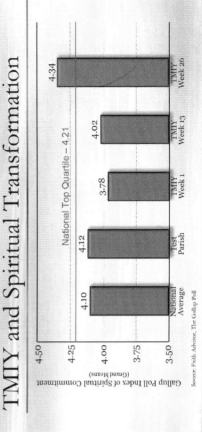

TMiY
THAT MAN IS YOU!
BECOMING A MAN AFTER GOD'S OWN HEART

We set a heroic goal this Fall:

Identify the path leading from sinner to saint!

Our next challenge is to walk this path!

TMIY and Spiritual Transformation

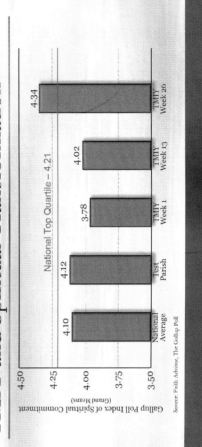

National Top Quartile – 4.21

| | National Average | Test Parish | TMIY Week 1 | TMIY Week 13 | TMIY Week 26 |
| | 4.10 | 4.12 | 3.78 | 4.02 | 4.34 |

Gallup Poll Index of Spiritual Commitment (Grand Means)

Source: Faith Advisor, The Gallup Poll

Nazareth and the Spiritual Life

7 Steps of That Man is You!

1. Honor your wedding vows.
2. Use money for others.
3. Give God some of your time.
4. Set your mind on the things above.
5. Find God in yourself.
6. Find God in other people.
7. Make it easy to be good and hard to be bad.

3 Stages of the Spiritual Life

1. Give away your body.
2. Give away your goods.   } Purgative Stage
3. Give away your time.
4. Receiving illumination from God.   } Illuminative Stage
5. Union with God in self.
6. Union with God through others.   } Unitive Stage
7. Ultimate union with God.

TMIY and Spiritual Transformation

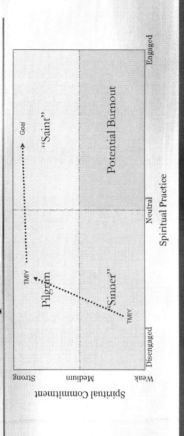

Chart:
- Y-axis: Spiritual Commitment (Weak, Medium, Strong)
- X-axis: Spiritual Practice (Disengaged, Neutral, Engaged)
- "Saint" → Goal
- Pilgrim (TMIY)
- "Sinner" (TMIY)
- Potential Burnout

TMIY and the Three Stages of the Interior Life

"What we humans call the beatitude of God is … full of continuous light and is perfect … It is purifying, illuminating, and perfecting."

1. Purgative: 84% of TMIY men.
   - Goal: Become less Selfish.
2. Illuminative: 14% of TMIY men.
   - Goal: Receive the light of Christ.
3. Unitive: 2% of TMIY men.
   - Goal: Live in profound union with God.

Source: "Pseudo-Dionysius – The Complete Works," The Classics of Western Spirituality, Paulist Press, New York, 1987, "Celestial Hierarchy," 3.2, p. 155.

Nazareth and the Spiritual Life

7 Steps of That Man is You!	3 Ages of the Spiritual Life	
1. Honor your wedding vows.	1. Give away your body.	Purgative Stage
2. Use money for others.	2. Give away your goods.	
3. Give God some of your time.	3. Give away your time.	
4. Set your mind on the things above.	4. Receiving illumination from God.	Illuminative Stage
5. Find God in yourself.	5. Union with God in self.	
6. Find God in other people.	6. Union with God through others.	Unitive Stage
7. Make it easy to be good and hard to be bad.	7. Ultimate union with God.	

That Man is You! has lit a fire!

We must allow this fire to "purge" the "old man" so that we truly become "A Man after God's own Heart."

Step 1: Encounter Christ

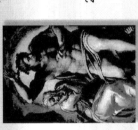

1. "Apart from me you can do nothing" (John 15:5).
   - "Come away" (Mark 6:31) with Christ. Silence external noise and give time to Christ.
   - Consecrate yourself to Christ, Our Lady or St. Joseph.
2. Make greater use of the sacraments.
   - Attend Mass as frequently as possible.
   - Return to or increase use of Confession.
3. Develop a robust prayer life.
   - Develop a rigorous, robust prayer life as discussed in Session 6: Give God some of Your Time.

Step 2: "Turn away from sin."

1. Get control of the media.
   - Avoid all content contrary to the faith and morals of the Church.
   - Set filters on all electronic equipment.
   - Reduce "neutral content" to release time to be used for spiritual practices.
2. Develop Holy Friendships
   - Avoid individuals who lead you away from God.
   - Develop holy friendships to lead you to God.
   - Reduce time spent in neutral friendships to have more time for spiritual life.

Step 3: "Embrace the Gospel."

1. Embrace appropriate ascetical practices.
   - Strengthen will by foregoing pleasurable things and doing things you dislike.
   - Historically alcohol and food are excellent choices.
   - Moderation is important.
2. Practice higher degrees of charity.
   - Use money as a tool for others.
   - Publically praise those who are difficult for you.
   - Allow yourself to be put lower than others.

Step 4: "It is not good for man to be alone."

1. Receive help and support from others.
   - Establish a buddy system: "Two are better than one … For if they fall, one will lift up his fellow; but woe to him who is alone, when he falls and has not another to lift him up" (Ecclesiastes 4:9-10).
   - TMIY Small Group.
   - Consider a 12-Step group.
   - Seek professional help.

We have put together a tool to help you develop and live the TMIY way of life.

The That Man is You! App.

Developing the Spirit of Nazareth

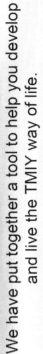

1. Communion
   - Spend as much time as possible together with your family: "It is not good for man to be alone" (Genesis 2:18).
   - Pray together with your family.
2. Ascetical Practices
   - Joyfully fulfill requests by wife and children for help.
   - Joyfully eat whatever is served. Take wife/children to restaurants they enjoy.
   - Give up personal pursuits/interests to spend time with family.
3. Love
   - Always think the best for others intentions.
   - Always speak well of others: "If anyone makes no mistakes in what he says, he is a perfect man" (James 3:2).

TMIY App: Web based App

- TMIY App is a web App running in a browser.
- Allows interactivity like "standard apps."
- Runs on all devices with HTML5.
- No need to download or reinstall new versions.
- Runs online reducing the danger of viruses, spyware and malware.
- Does not take up space on your device.
- Most massive companies have been using "web apps" on their websites while still developing "standard apps" for mobile devices.
- sonarDesign allows us to design once and reach all TMIY participants (150 different devices).

TMIY App: Cutting Edge Technology

- sonarDesign: New technology company started by the former COO of EA Sports and the man who developed the guidance system for the space shuttle.
- Web APP running in HTML5.
- Google and the major technology players mandated that HTML5 as the only constant across all modern devices anticipating it would become the basis for integrating mobile world.
- sonarDesign solved the issue so that their products run across all platforms/devices.
- Google has invited sonarDesign for conferences

TMIY App: Materials at your Fingertips

- Delivery of TMIY content.
  - ✓ Watch TMIY Sessions.
  - ✓ Read TMIY PowerPoints
- Availability of Traditional Catholic Prayers:
  - ✓ The Rosary.
  - ✓ The Way of the Cross.
  - ✓ Examination of Conscience.
  - ✓ Many additional prayers.
- Ability to find a TMIY program anywhere in the country.

TMIY App: Cutting Edge Spiritually

- Opportunity to develop customized spiritual plan-of-life.
- Survey questions on the 7 Covenants of TMIY.
- Personalized demographic data.
- Multiple options for increased flexibility.
- Consistent with materials and methodology of Year 2: Apostles of a New Springtime.
- Designed by Steve Bollman personally.

Accessing the TMIY App

- You may access the app either through a link on the TMIY website or through the email we send you.
- The sonar website will do a compatibility test of your device.
- Click "continue" to proceed into the app.
- Click on "register now."
- Enter your email and password, which is different than your TMIY password. Click on confirm.
- Click on "I agree to sonar terms."
- Click "Register."
- Click "Login" and enter your email and password.

I'd like to walk you through the three most important steps to begin using the app. After the session, you'll be able to find all of these on our website.

Creating a Spiritual Plan of Life

1. Take Surveys
   - Click on "Profile". Enter information. Click "Save"
   - Click "Go to Surveys."
   - Click on one of the surveys. Read introduction. Click "Yes"
   - Answer all questions. Read box. Click "Continue"
   - Answer surveys questions for all covenants.
   - Click "Continue" to access "Plan-of-Life" screen.
2. Setup Plan of Life by selecting TMiYs
   - Click on "+" at bottom.
   - Select covenant. Select TMiY to review.
   - Select "+ Add to Plan of Life
   - Repeat for all Covenants.

Small Group Discussion

Starter Questions

1. Where are you on the four quadrants – saint, sinner, pilgrim or burnout?
2. How will you finalize your spiritual plan-of-life before Christmas?

Next Week
Set out into the Deep

Adding the TMIY App Tile to Device

- Login to the TMIY App using your email and password.
- Click on the "add a tile button" below the "Settings" button at the bottom of the app.
- Click on the "Add to Home Screen" button.

- Name App.
- Press "Add" to add the TMIY Tile to your screen.
- Position TMIY Tile to be easily accessed.

Creating a Spiritual Plan of Life

3. Set Reminders
   - Click on "Settings" at the bottom of the App.
   - Set time for reminder by clicking on 4 boxes.
   - Set mode to receive reminder and provide information.
4. Check in Daily
   - Check the box next to the TMiY each day you complete it.
   - At the end of the day, save the data by clicking the save TMiY information button.
   - Clear TMiY check marks by clicking the button on the bottom far right.
   - Check progress by clicking the calendar.

SESSION 12

The Journey to Nazareth

TMIY
THAT MAN IS YOU!
BECOMING A MAN AFTER GOD'S OWN HEART

We have begun a long and arduous journey.

We must recognize the challenges that await us.

TMIY and Spiritual Transformation

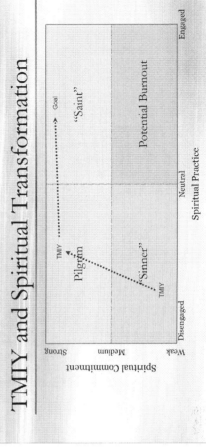

Goal → "Saint"

TMIY

Pilgrim

"Sinner"

TMIY

Potential Burnout

Strong / Medium / Weak — Spiritual Commitment

Disengaged / Neutral / Engaged — Spiritual Practice

TMIY and the Three Stages of the Interior Life

"What we humans call the beatitude of God is … full of continuous light and is perfect …. It is purifying, illuminating, and perfecting."

1. Purgative: 84% of TMIY men.
   - Goal: Become less Selfish.
2. Illuminative: 14% of TMIY men.
   - Goal: Receive the light of Christ.
3. Unitive: 2% of TMIY men.
   - Goal: Live in profound union with God.

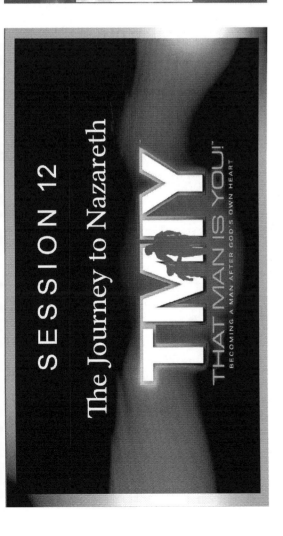

Source: "Pseudo-Dionysius – The Complete Works," The Classics of Western Spirituality, Paulist Press, New York, 1987, "Celestial Hierarchy," 3.2, p. 155.

Christ provides us with two important tools so that we may complete this journey.

Spiritual food and spiritual companions.

The Word of God

- "The tempter came and said to him, 'If you are the Son of God, command these stones to become loaves of bread.' But he answered, 'It is written "Man shall not live by bread alone, but by every word that proceeds from the mouth of God"'" (Matthew 4:4).

- "You search the Scriptures, because you think that in them you have eternal life; and it is they that bear witness to me" (John 5:39).

The Challenge of the Spiritual Life

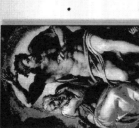

- "We are not contending against flesh and blood, but against the principalities, against the powers, against the world rulers of this present darkness, against the spiritual hosts of wickedness in the heavenly places" (Ephesians 6:12).

- "Which of you, desiring to build a tower, does not first sit down and count the cost, whether he has enough to complete it? Otherwise, when he has laid a foundation, and is not able to finish, all who see it begin to mock him" (Luke 14:28-29).

- "Many have tried to return to you, and have not had the strength in themselves to achieve it" (St. Augustine, Confessions 10.42).

Source: St. Augustine, "Confessions," Book 10, ala-xlu, Trans. Chadwick, H. Oxford World's Classics, Oxford University Press, 2008.

Spiritual Food for the Journey

- The Word of God: "Man shall not live by bread alone, but by every word that proceeds from the mouth of God" (Matthew 4:4).

- The Will of God: "My food is to do the will of him who sent me, and to accomplish his work" (John 4:34).

- The Eucharist: "My flesh is food indeed, and my blood is drink indeed" (John 6:55).

The Will of God

- "Meanwhile the disciples besought him, saying, 'Rabbi, eat.' But he said to them, 'I have food to eat of which you do not know … My food is to do the will of him who sent me, and to accomplish his work'" (John 4:31-34).

- "This is the will of God, your sanctification" (1 Thessalonians 4:3).

- Holy (קָדוֹשׁ) → qadosh
- Consecrated (קָדַשׁ) → qadash
- To be set aside (קֹדֶשׁ) → qodesh

Practicing Lectio Divina

1. Lectio or Reading
2. Meditatio or Meditation
3. Oratio or Prayer
4. Contemplatio or Contemplation

The Plan of Life as a Pathway to Holiness

1. Practical and systematic approach to spiritual life.
2. Life as husbands and fathers – the Spirit of Nazareth.
3. Encounter Christ
   - Find God in family members.
   - Pray together with your family members.
4. "Turn away from sin"
   - Minimize media – give time to family.
   - Ascetical practices – place self and desires below family members
5. "Embrace the Gospel"
   - Higher levels of charity – use money for others.
   - Help family members succeed.
6. Communion: "God is found in communion."
7. Plan of Life – TMIY App

The Sanctification of Marriage

"How can I ever express the happiness of the marriage that is joined together by the Church, strengthened by an offering, sealed by a blessing, announced by angels and ratified by the Father? … How wonderful the bond between two believers, with a single hope, a single desire, a single observance, a single service! They are both brethren and both fellow-servants; there is no separation between them in spirit or flesh; in fact they are truly two in one flesh, and where the flesh is one, one is the spirit."

Tertullian

Ad Uxoren, II, VIII, 6-8

Bread for the Journey

"Having passed from this world to the Father, Christ gives us in the Eucharist the pledge of glory with him. Participation in the Holy Sacrifice identifies us with his Heart, sustains our strength along the pilgrimage of this life, makes us long for eternal life, and unites us even now to the Church in heaven, the Blessed Virgin Mary, and all the saints."

Catechism #1419

The Eucharist

"Our fathers ate the manna in the wilderness … Jesus then said to them, 'Truly, truly, I say to you, it was not Moses who gave you the bread from heaven; my Father gives you the true bread from heaven … I am the living bread which came down from heaven; if any one eats of this bread, he will live for ever; and the bread which I shall give for the life of the world is my flesh … For my flesh is food indeed, and my blood is drink indeed." (John 6:31-55).

God feeds us with spiritual food on our pilgrimage to him.

He also provides us with companions for the journey.

The Practice of the Presence of God

"I cannot express to you what is taking place in me at present … I devote myself exclusively to remaining always in his holy presence. I keep myself in his presence by simple attentiveness and a general loving awareness of God that I call 'actual presence of God' or better, a quiet and secret conversation of the soul with God that is lasting."

Brother Lawrence

The TMIY Small Group

- "Two are better than one … For if they fall, one will lift up his fellow; but woe to him who is alone, when he falls and has not another to lift him up" (Ecclesiastes 4:9-10).
- Established group of spiritual companions.
- Share a common template for attaining holiness – 7 Steps of TMIY.

Companions for the Journey

"The Lord appointed seventy others, and sent them on ahead of him, two by two, into every town and place where he himself was to come. And he said to them … 'Go your way; behold, I send you out as lambs in the midst of wolves' … The seventy returned with joy, saying, 'Lord, even the demons are subject to us in your name!' And he said to them, 'I saw Satan fall like lightning from heaven. Behold, I have given you authority to tread upon serpents and scorpions, and over all the power of the enemy; and nothing shall hurt you. Nevertheless do not rejoice in this … but rejoice that your names are written in heaven" (Luke 10:1-20).

An Ongoing Journey

- As long as the small group uses the shared spiritual template of the 7 Steps, they have the framework to progress in the journey beyond the confines of the TMIY weekly meeting.
- Many groups continue over the summer.
- TMIY will provide a list of approved/suggested materials to help men better live the 7 Steps.

Holiness and the TMIY Small Group

- Progress on spiritual plan-of-life to help the members feed on holiness.
- Questions from session, which always include Scripture and teachings of the faith, to help the members feed on the Word of God.
- Challenge to attend Mass together as a group once per month to feed on the Eucharist.

Pray for Laborers in the Vineyard

> I tell you, lift up your eyes, and see how the fields are already white for harvest. The harvest is plentiful, but the laborers are few; pray therefore the Lord of the harvest to send out laborers into his harvest.

John 4:35 and Luke 10:2

Small Group Discussion

Starter Questions

1. How will your small group join together to feed on the Word, the Will and the Eucharist?
2. Who would be good spiritual mentors and leaders in your parish?

Next Week
Discerning the Call of God

The Need for Spiritual Mentors

- Ideally, parish would have a person designated as the spiritual mentor.
- We would like to work with him to enter more deeply into the spiritual depth of the 7 Steps.
- We would like you to help identify and nominate a spiritual mentor in your parish.
- The spiritual mentor would work with the leaders of each small group to guide them on their journey.

The Call for Apostles

"Let us go forward in hope! A new millennium is opening before the Church like a vast ocean upon which we shall venture ... we need ... a generous heart to become the instruments of his work ... Christ ... bids us to set out once more on our journey ... The missionary mandate accompanies us into the Third Millennium and urges us to share the enthusiasm of the very first Christians; we can count on the power of the same Spirit who was poured out at Pentecost and who impels us still today to start out anew."

Novo Millennio Ineunte #58

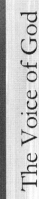

SESSION 13

To Hear the Voice of God

TMIY
THAT MAN IS YOU!
BECOMING A MAN AFTER GOD'S OWN HEART

"

Jesus Christ personally invited you to be here today. You said, 'Yes.' And I thank you.

"

The Voice of God

"Conscience is the most secret core and sanctuary of a man. There he is alone with God, Whose voice echoes in his depths."

Second Vatican Council
Gaudium et Spes, #16

The Call of That Man is You!

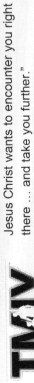

TMIY
THAT MAN IS YOU!
BECOMING A MAN AFTER GOD'S OWN HEART

- "Wherever you are in your spiritual life, Jesus Christ wants to encounter you right there … and take you further."

- "That Man is You! is about a personal encounter with Jesus Christ so that Jesus Christ can transform your life."

The Call to become a Member of Christ

- "Baptism makes the neophyte 'a new creature,' and adopted son of God, who has become a 'partaker of the divine nature,' member of Christ and co-heir with him, and a temple of the Holy Spirit" (Catechism #1265).

- "The sacrament of marriage ... takes up again and makes specific the sanctifying grace of Baptism ... spouses are made part [of the mystery of the death and Resurrection of Christ] in a new way" (St. Pope John Paul II, Familiaris Consortio, #56).

Mother Teresa of Calcutta

- 1910: Born August 26 in Albania.
- 1916: First communion/confirmation.
- 1918: Death of her father.
- 1928: Joins Sisters of Loreto in Ireland.
- 1929: Arrives in India.
- 1946: Inspiration on September 10th.
- 1948: Enters slums on August 17th.
- 1950: Missionaries of Charity.
- 1979: Noble Peace Prize
- 1997: Dies on September 5th.
- 2003: Beatified on October 20th.

The Universal Call to Holiness

- "God desires all men to be saved and to come to the knowledge of the truth" (1 Timothy 2:4).

- "This is the will of God, your sanctification" (1 Thessalonians 4:3).

- God desires every person on earth to go straight to heaven.

Every person is called to be holy within their state in life. For most men this will entail become holy as a husband and father. Is there something more?

The Hidden Face of Christ

- "Truly, I say to you, as you did it to one of the least of my brethren, you did it to me" (Matthew 25:40).
- "They are Jesus. Each one is Jesus in a distressing disguise" (Mother Teresa).

A call is an initiative by God to which we respond. Since men love to be the initiators, we have trouble allowing God to take the lead.

What does a call look like?

A Call within a Call

"You have become my Spouse for my Love – you have come to India for Me. The thirst you had for souls brought you so far. Are you afraid to take one more step for your Spouse – for me – for souls? Is your generosity grown cold – am I a second to you?"

Jesus to Mother Teresa

An Encounter with Christ

- "We are not social workers. We may be doing social work in the eyes of some people, but we must be contemplatives in the heart of the world."
- "For me it is so clear – everything in the Missionaries of Charity exists only to satiate Jesus. His words on the wall of every Missionaries of Charity chapel, they are not from [the] past only, but alive here and now, spoken to you."

The Call of St. Matthew

"As Jesus passed on from there, he saw a man called Matthew sitting at the tax office; and he said to him, 'Follow me.' And he rose and followed him. And as he sat at table in the house behold, many tax collectors and sinners came and sat down with Jesus and his disciples. And when the Pharisees saw this, they said to his disciples, 'Why does your teacher eat with tax collectors and sinners?' But when he heard it, he said, 'Those who are well have no need of a physician, but those who are sick. Go and learn what this means, 'I desire mercy, and not sacrifice.' For I came not to call the righteous, but sinners'" (Matthew 9:9-13).

The Call of St. Paul

"As Saul journeyed he approached Damascus, and suddenly a light from heaven flashed about him. And he fell to the ground and heard a voice saying to him, 'Saul, Saul, why do you persecute me?' And he said, 'Who are you, Lord?' And he said, 'I am Jesus, whom you are persecuting; but rise and enter the city, and you will be told what you are to do' ... Saul arose from the ground; and when his eyes were opened, he could see nothing; so they led him by the band and brought him into Damascus. And for three days he was without sight, and neither ate nor drank."

Acts 9:3-9

Not surprisingly, many men miss the call of God because they do not recognize his voice. I know that I struggled to discern God's voice.

The Call of St. Peter

"One of the two who heard John speak, and followed him, was Andrew, Simon Peter's brother. He first found his brother Simon, and said to him, 'We have found the Messiah' ... He brought him to Jesus. Jesus looked at him, and said, 'So you are Simon the son of John? You shall be called Cephas' (which means Peter)."

John 1:40-42

The Call of Samuel

"Then the Lord called, 'Samuel! Samuel!' and he said, 'Here I am!' and ran to Eli, and said, 'Here I am, for you called me.' But he said, 'I did not call; lie down again.'"

1 Samuel 3:4-5

The Answer of Samuel

"Then Eli perceived that the Lord was calling the boy. Therefore Eli said to Samuel, 'Go, lie down; and if he calls you, you shall say, 'Speak, Lord, for they servants hears.' So Samuel went and lay down in his place. And the Lord came and stood forth, calling as at other times, 'Samuel! Samuel!' And Samuel said, 'Speak, for they servant hears.'"

1 Samuel 3:48-10

The Still, Small Voice of God

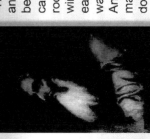

"The word of the Lord came to Elijah saying, 'Go forth and stand upon the mount before the Lord; and behold the Lord shall pass. And a great strong wind came overthrowing the mountains and breaking the rocks, but the Lord was not in the wind. After the wind, an earthquake, but the Lord was not in the earthquake. After the earthquake, a fire, but the Lord was not in the fire. After the fire, a still small voice. And when Elijah heard it, he covered his face with his mantle. And the voice said to Elijah, 'What are you doing here?'"

1 Kings 19:9-13

Ultimately, this is the challenge of the spiritual life – listen to God. As we have seen, God calls in more than one way. We must harmonize two very important realities.

God Speaks to the Heart

"The Father will give you another Counselor, to be with you for ever, even the Spirit of truth … you know him, for he dwells with you, and will be in you."

John 14:16-17

Small Group Discussion

Starter Questions

1. Do you know God's plan for your life?
2. When have you most clearly heard the voice of God?

Next Week

The World in which we Live.

God Speaks through the Church

"He who hears you hears me, and he who rejects you rejects me."

Luke 10:16

Our task this Spring is easy. Listen to God. Many of you will hear a call. Before we are done, you will have the chance to answer that call.

SESSION 14

The World in which we Live

TMIY
THAT MAN IS YOU!
BECOMING A MAN AFTER GOD'S OWN HEART

You were created to live in this moment in time. It establishes the context for your call.

The Church helps us to clearly understand this context.

Your First Call

- "Before I formed you in the womb I knew you, and before you were born I consecrated you" (Jeremiah 1:5).

- "Thus says the Lord, he who created you, O Jacob, he who formed you, O Israel: 'Fear not, for I have redeemed you; I have called you by name, you are mine'" (Isaiah 43:1).

Pope Leo XIII: October 13, 1884

"Pope Leo XIII was attending Mass [when] suddenly we saw him raise his head and stare at something above the celebrant's head. He was staring motionlessly, without batting an eye. His expression was one of horror and awe; the color and look on his face changing rapidly ... Leo XIII truly saw in a vision demonic spirits who were congregating on the Eternal City (Rome)."

Father Gabriele Amorth
An Exorcist Tells his Story

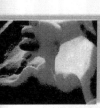

Pope Pius XI: May 8, 1928

"These things in truth are so sad that you might say that such events foreshadow and portend the 'beginning of sorrows,' that is to say of those that shall be brought by the man of sin, 'who lifted up above all that is called God or is worshipped' (2 Thes 2:4)"

Miserentissimus Redemptor
May 8, 1928

Blessed Pope Paul VI: June 29, 1972

"The smoke of Satan has entered the sanctuary of God through some crack or small fissure."

June 29, 1972

St. Pope John Paul II

- "We are in fact faced by an objective 'conspiracy against life'" (Evangelium Vitae, #17).

- "The evil of the twentieth century was not a small-scale evil, it was not simply 'homemade.' It was an evil of gigantic proportions" (*Memory and Identity*).

- "It is legitimate and even necessary to ask whether [the socioeconomic system of the West] is not the work of another ideology of evil, more subtle and hidden, perhaps, intent upon exploiting human rights themselves against man and against the family" (Memory and Identity).

Pope Benedict XVI: April 18, 2005

- "Today, having a clear faith based on the Creed of the Church is often labeled as fundamentalism ... We are building a dictatorship of relativism" (Cardinal Ratzinger, April 18, 2005).

- "The pollution of the outward environment that we are witnessing is only the mirror and the consequence of the pollution of the inward environment ... And we hear the groaning of creation as we have never heard it before" (Cardinal Ratzinger, 1996).

The Spiritual Reality of the Fall

- "Sin and death have entered into man's history in some way through the very heart of that unity that had from the 'beginning' been formed by the man and woman, created and called to become 'one flesh'" (Pope John Paul II, March 5, 1980).
- "... in human history the 'rays of fatherhood' meet a first resistance in the obscure but real fact of original sin. This is truly the key for interpreting reality ... Original sin attempts, then, to abolish fatherhood" (Pope John Paul II, *Crossing the Threshold of Hope*).

The family is placed at the heart of the great struggle between good and evil, between life and death, between love and all that is opposed to love.

Pope John Paul II
Letter to Families, #23

Simone De Beauvoir

- January 9, 1908 – April 14, 1986.
- Jean Paul Sartre's love interest for 50 years.
- Transitions Jean Paul Sartre's philosophy into a basis for radical feminism: The Second Sex.
- "The worst curse that was laid upon woman was that she should be excluded from those warlike forays. For it is not in giving life but in risking life that man is raised above the animal; that is why superiority has been accorded in humanity not to the sex that brings forth but to that which kills."
- "No woman should be authorized to stay at home to raise her children. Women should not have that choice ... as long as the family and the myth of the family and the myth of maternity and the maternal instinct are not destroyed, women will still be oppressed."

Jean Paul Sartre

- June 21, 1905 – April 15, 1980.
- Incredibly popular French existentialist philosopher and playwright.
- "If God exists, man is nothing; if man exists ... God does not exist ... He does not exist ... Joy, tears of joy. Alleluia! I have liberated us. No more Heaven, no more Hell."
- Love is IMPOSSIBLE: "While I attempt to free myself from the hold of the other, the other is trying to free himself from mine; while I seek to enslave the other, the other seeks to enslave me ... Conflict is the original meaning of being-for-others."
- "Hell is other people."

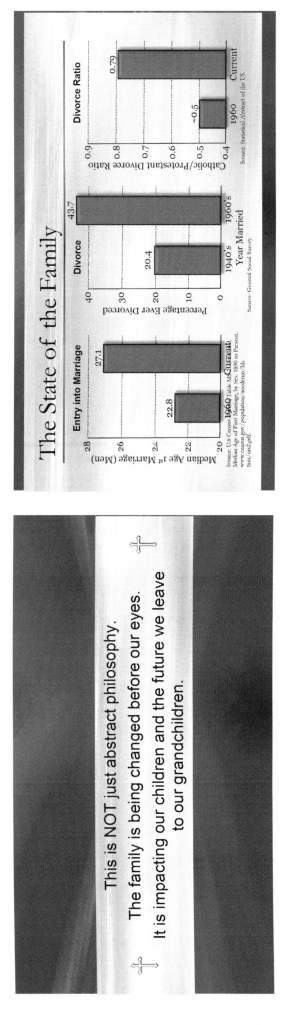

The State of the Family

Entry into Marriage — Median Age 1st Marriage (Men)
- 1960: 22.8
- Current: 27.1

Source: US Census 1960 Table MS-2 Current Median Age of First Marriage, by Sex: 1890 to Present. www.census.gov/population/socdemo/hh fam/ms2.pdf

Divorce — Percentage Ever Divorced (Year Married)
- 1940's: 20.4
- 1960's: 43.7

Source: General Social Survey.

Divorce Ratio — Catholic/Protestant Divorce Ratio
- 1960: ~0.5
- Current: 0.79

Source: Statistical Abstract of the US.

The Pain of Children

Abortions — Percentage of Conceptions Aborted
- 1960: <1
- Current: ~22

Source: Statistical Abstract of the U.S.

Illegitimate Births — Percentage Illegitimate Births
- 1960: 5.3
- Current: 40.7

Source: Statistical Abstract of the US. Vital Statistics of the US

Children with Parents — Marriages Ending in Divorce (%)
- 1960: 73
- Current: 46

Source: Pew Research Center, "Less than half of U.S. kids today live in a 'traditional family,'" December 22, 2014.

This is NOT just abstract philosophy.

The family is being changed before our eyes.

It is impacting our children and the future we leave to our grandchildren.

The State of the Family

Married Households — Percentage of Married Households
- 1960: 74.4
- Current: 49.7

Source: Statistical Abstract of the US.

Traditional Families — Percentage "Traditional Family"
- 1960: 44.2
- Current: 20.9

Source: Statistical Abstract of the US.

Single Families — Single Family Households (%)
- 1960: 4.4
- Current: 9.1

Source: Statistical Abstract of the US.

The Death of the European Culture

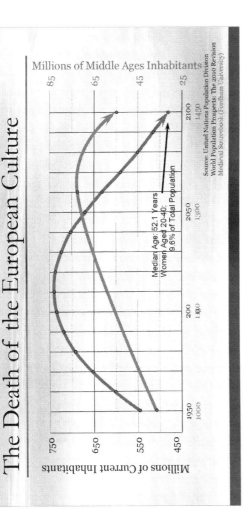

Millions of Current Inhabitants

Millions of Middle Ages Inhabitants

Median Age: 52.1 Years
Women Aged 20-40:
9.6% of Total Population

Source: United Nations Population Division
World Population Prospects: The 2010 Revision
Medieval Sourcebook (Fordham University)

The Pain of Children

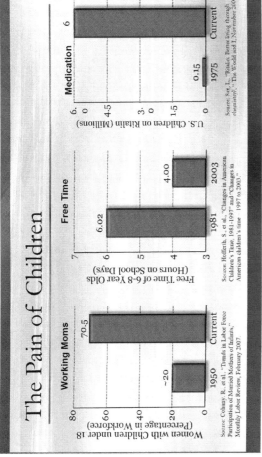

Working Moms

Women with Children under 18
(Percentage in Workforce)

~20   1950
70.5   Current

Source: Cohany, R., et al., "Trends in Labor Force
Participation of Married Mothers of Infants,"
Monthly Labor Review, February 2007.

Free Time

Free Time of 6-8 Year Olds
(Hours on School Days)

6.02   1981
4.00   2003

Source: Hofferth, S., et al., "Changes in American
Children's Time, 1981-1997" and "Changes in
American children's time 1997 to 2003."

Medication

U.S. Children on Ritalin (Millions)

0.15   1975
6   Current

Source: Say, L., "Ritalin: Better living through
chemistry", The World and I, November 2000.

Freedom from Maternity

"The Platform for Action is an agenda for women's empowerment. It aims … at removing all the obstacles to women's active participation in all spheres of public and private life through a full and equal share in economic, social, cultural and political decision-making … Maternity, motherhood, parenting and the role of women in procreation must not be a basis for discrimination nor restrict the full participation of women in society."

United Nations 4th World Conference on Women
Beijing, China, September 4-15, 1995
Conference Report, #1, #29

Although Western culture is entering into a "demographic winter," international organizations see it as their mission to continue to promote unlimited access to birth control and abortion.

A New "Freedom" for Modern Culture

"For two decades of economic and social developments, people have organized intimate relationships and made choices that define their views of themselves and their places in society, in reliance on the availability of abortion in the event that contraception should fail. The ability of women to participate equally in the economic and social life of the Nation has been facilitated by their ability to control their reproductive lives."

United States Supreme Court
Planned Parenthood v. Casey, 1992

The Path to Equality

"Survey data suggest that approximately 120 million additional women world wide would be currently using a modern family-planning method if more accurate information and affordable service were easily available. These numbers do not include the substantial and growing numbers of sexually active unmarried individuals wanting and in need of information and services ... To meet their needs and close the existing large gaps in services, family planning and contraceptive supplies will need to expand very rapidly over the next several years ... All countries should take steps ... by the year 2015 to provide universal access to a full range of safe and reliable family-planning methods."

International Conference on Population and Development
Cairo, Egypt September 5-13, 1994
Plan of Action, Chapter 7

Small Group Discussion

Starter Questions

1. How can you stay more informed about the statements from the Holy Father?
2. How are you doing on your Spiritual Plan of Life?

Next Week

The Promise of Springtime

We live in dramatic moments.

God knew this was your destiny.

God created you specifically for this moment.

SESSION 15

The Promise of Springtime

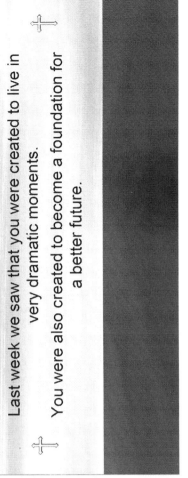

TMIY
THAT MAN IS YOU!
BECOMING A MAN AFTER GOD'S OWN HEART

Last week we saw that you were created to live in very dramatic moments.

You were also created to become a foundation for a better future.

For over 50 years the Church has been pointing us to a new springtime, which is built upon the renewal of the Christian family.

A New Springtime for Christianity

- "I see the dawning of a new missionary age, which will become a radiant day bearing an abundant harvest ... As the third millennium of the redemption draws near, God is preparing a great springtime for Christianity" (Pope John Paul II, *Redemptoris Missio*, #92 and #86).

- "I implore Mary, the heavenly Mother of the Church, to be so good as to devote herself to this prayer of humanity's new Advent ... I hope that through this prayer we shall be able to receive the Holy Spirit coming upon us and thus become Christ's witnesses "to the ends of the earth" (Redemptor Hominis, #22).

The Second Vatican Council

- "The family is, so to speak, the domestic church" (Vatican II, *Lumen Gentium*, #11).
- "The family ... is the foundation of society" (Vatican II, *Gaudium et Spes*, #52).
- "God has judged [marriage] worthy of special gifts, healing, perfecting and exalting gifts of grace and charity" (Vatican II, *Gaudium et Spes*, #49).

St Pope John Paul II and the Family

- Begins Pontificate with catechesis on marriage – The Theology of the Body.
- Assassination attempt on May 13, 1981 while on the way to found the Pontifical Academy of the Family. Feast of Our Lady of Fatima, which ends with a vision of the Holy Family.
- "Future of the world and of the Church passes through the family."
- "The family is placed at the heart of the great struggle between good and evil, between life and death and between love and all that is opposed to love."
- Offers his suffering for the family.

St. Pope John XXIII

- "Renew in our own days your miracles as of a second Pentecost" (St. Pope John XXIII, Preparatory Prayer for Vatican II).
- St. Pope John XXIII travels to Loretto on October 4, 1962.
- In the "holy house" at Loretto, he entrusts the Second Vatican Council to Our Lady.

Blessed Pope Paul VI and Nazareth

- Blessed Pope Paul VI becomes first modern Pope to travel to the Holy Land in 1964.
- "Nazareth is a kind of school where we may begin to discover what Christ's life was like and even to understand his Gospel ... Here everything speaks to us, everything has meaning ... How I would like to return to my childhood and attend the simple yet profound school that is Nazareth!" (Blessed Pope Paul VI, Address at the Basilica of the Annunciation, January 5, 1964).

Pope Benedict XVI: Family as Gospel

- Deus Caritas Est: "Love is indeed 'ecstasy', not in the sense of a moment of intoxication, but rather as a journey, an ongoing exodus out of the closed inward-looking self towards its liberation through self-giving, and thus towards authentic self-discovery and indeed the discovery of God" (Deus Caritas Est, #6).
- "The word of God [from the Book of Sirach] presents the family as the first school of wisdom" (Homily, Mass at Nazareth, May 15, 2009).
- "Matrimony is a Gospel in itself" (October 7, 2012).

Pope Francis: Swim against the Tide

- Papal crest has symbols for Jesus, Mary and Joseph –the Holy Family. Begins ministry on Feast of St. Joseph. Consecrates ministry to Our Lady of Fatima.
- "I ask you to swim against the tide; yes, I am asking you to rebel against this culture that sees everything as temporary and that ultimately believes you are incapable of responsibility, that believes you are incapable of true love" (Pope Francis, Meeting with Volunteers of WYD, July 28, 2013).

A Light for our Homes

"The essence and role of the family are in the final analysis specified by love … This being the case, it is in the Holy Family, the original 'Church in miniature (*Ecclesia Domestica*), that every Christian family must be reflected. 'Through God's mysterious design, it was in that family that the Son of God spent long years of a hidden life. It is therefore the prototype and example for all Christian families.'"

St. John Paul II, Redemptoris Custos, #7

✠ The new springtime of the Church will be tied to the family, which is called to participate in the life of the Holy Family. As such, we must journey to Nazareth. ✠

The Temple at Nazareth

- "Jesus went down with them and came to Nazareth, and was obedient to them … And Jesus increased in wisdom and in stature, and in favor with God and man" (Luke 2:52).
- "Samuel continued to grow both in stature and in favor with the Lord and with men" (1 Samuel 2:26).
- "The secrets Mary had been in charge of revealing to Jesus, secrets wrapped in silence and darkness. Instead of opposing the one he called 'my Father' against the carpenter of Nazareth, Jesus, on the threshold of his conscious adolescence, had to see them both together in the same glance" (Fr. Andrew Doze).

Source: Doze, Fr. Andrew, "Saint Joseph: The Shadow of the Father," Trans. Audett, F., Alba House, New York, 1992, p. 67.

The Temple of God

"Now his parents went to Jerusalem every year at the feast of Passover. And when he was twelve years old … and when the feast was ended … the boy Jesus stayed behind in Jerusalem … supposing him to be in the company they went a day's journey … and when they did not find him, they returned to Jerusalem, seeking him. After three days they found him in the temple … and his mother said to him, 'Son, why have you treated us so? Behold, your father and I have been looking for you anxiously.' And he said to them … 'Did you not know that I must be in my Fathers house?'"

Luke 2:41-51

The Home of St. Joseph at Nazareth

- The Holy Family "was a heaven, a paradise on earth, endless delights in this place of grief; it was a glory already begun in the vileness, abjection and lowliness of their life" (Monsignor Jean Jacques Olier).
- "Then I saw a new heaven and a new earth … 'Behold, the dwelling of God is with men … he will wipe away every tear from their eyes, and death shall be no more, neither shall there be mourning nor crying nor pain any more … But nothing unclean shall enter it, nor any one who practices abomination or falsehood, but only those who are written in the Lamb's book of life'" (Revelation 21:1-27).

Source: Doze, Fr. Andrew, "Saint Joseph, The Shadow of the Father," Trans. Audett, F., Alba House, New York, 1992, p. 52.

The Holy Family is the Temple of God. It is the original ecclesia domestica. We must enter into this mystery to better understand our own homes.

The Importance of the Holy Family

"In this great undertaking, which is the renewal of all things in Christ, marriage ...becomes a new reality ... We see that at the beginning of the New Testament, as at the beginning of the Old, there is a married couple. But whereas Adam and Eve were the source of evil which was unleashed on the world, Joseph and Mary are the summit from which holiness spreads over all the earth."

St. Pope John Paul II
Redemptoris Custos, #7

The Life of Nazareth

- "O Mary Immaculate, O glorious Joseph! And you, St. John, beloved disciple of the Divine Heart, teach me the great science of love."

- "I know, O Mother full of grace, that you lived in great poverty in Nazareth. You did not long to leave it; no raptures, miracles or ecstasies lightened your life ... you chose to tread the everyday paths so as to show little ones the way to heaven."

- "I applied myself to practicing little virtues, not having the capability of practicing the great."

Source: Doze, Fr. Andrew, "Saint Joseph: The Shadow of the Father," Taus Audett, F., Alba House, New York, 1992, p. 68.
Quoted in Longenecker, D. "St. Benedict and St. Therese: The Little Rule and the Little Way," One Sunday Visitor Publishing Division, 2002, p. 175.
"Story of a Soul: The Autobiography of St. Therese of Lisieux," 3rd Edition, Translated by Clarke, J., ICS Publications, 1996, p. 159.

The Mystery of Paradise

1. Vision of the Face of God:
   - "The admirable St. Joseph was given to the earth to express the adorable perfection of God the Father in a tangible way" (Monsignor Jean Jacques Olier).
2. Evil remains on the outside:
   - Jesus is the Word Incarnate (Cf. John 1:14).
   - Mary is the Immaculate Conception (Cf. Luke 1:28).
   - Joseph is the just man in Scripture (Cf. Matthew 1:19).
3. No more death or sorrow:
   - "Jesus, crying with a loud voice, said, 'Father, into thy hands I commit my spirit!' And having said this he breathed his last" (Luke 23:46).
   - "Son, why have you treated us so? Behold, your father and I have been looking for you anxiously" (Luke 2:48).

Source: Doze, Fr. Andrew, "Saint Joseph: The Shadow of the Father," Taus Audett, F., Alba House, New York, 1992, p. 51.

We must make the journey to Nazareth.

Fortunately, we have saints to point the way.

The transformation of your home is within reach.

Seven Steps to a Superabundant Marriage

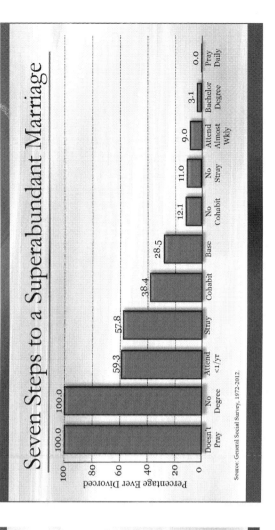

Chart: Percentage Ever Divorced

Doesn't Pray / No Degree	100.0
No Degree	100.0
Attend <1/yr	59.3
Stray	57.8
Cohabit	38.4
Base	28.5
No Cohabit	12.1
No Stray	11.0
Attend Almost Wkly	9.0
Bachelor Degree	3.1
Pray Daily	0.0

Source: General Social Survey, 1972-2012.

Small Group Discussion

Starter Questions

1. How can your home better reflect its dignity as a Temple of God?
2. How can you live the seven steps as a means of entering into the life of the Holy Family?

Next Week

Apostles of a New Springtime

The Life of Nazareth

Holy Family at Nazareth

1. The Niddah Laws on sexual purity (Cf. Leviticus 15:19ff).
2. The separation of the Challah (Cf. Numbers 15:20).
3. The Nerot Laws (Exodus 20:8).
4. The angel is sent to Mary and Joseph to open their minds.
5. Mary finds God in self.
6. Joseph finds God in Mary.
7. The Christian home is born of mercy.

Paradisus Dei

1. Honor your wedding vows.
2. Use money for others.
3. Give God some of your time.
4. Set your mind on the things above.
5. Find God in yourself.
6. Find God in other people.
7. Make it easy to be good and hard to be bad.

Our homes can truly share in the mystery of Nazareth.

Nonetheless, there are great obstacles.

SESSION 16

Apostles of the Family

TMIY

THAT MAN IS YOU!

BECOMING A MAN AFTER GOD'S OWN HEART

We have been promised a new springtime. For this to become a reality, we must journey to Nazareth and live the life of the Holy Family.

A New Springtime for Christianity

- "I see the dawning of a new missionary age, which will become a radiant day bearing an abundant harvest ... As the third millennium of the redemption draws near, God is preparing a great springtime for Christianity" (Pope John Paul II, *Redemptoris Missio*, #92 and #86).

- "I implore Mary, the heavenly Mother of the Church, to be so good as to devote herself to this prayer of humanity's new Advent ... I hope that through this prayer we shall be able to receive the Holy Spirit coming upon us and thus become Christ's witnesses 'to the ends of the earth'" (Redemptor Hominis, #22).

The Importance of the Holy Family

"In this great undertaking, which is the renewal of all things in Christ, marriage ... becomes a new reality ... We see that at the beginning of the New Testament, as at the beginning of the Old, there is a married couple. But whereas Adam and Eve were the source of evil which was unleashed on the world, Joseph and Mary are the summit from which holiness spreads over all the earth."

St. Pope John Paul II
Redemptoris Custos, #7

The Miraculous Medal Apparition

"The times are very evil. Sorrows will come upon France; the throne will be overturned. The whole world will be upset by miseries of every kind … There will be an abundance of sorrows; and the danger will be great. Yet do not be afraid … I shall be with you myself … I will grant you many graces … The moment will come when the danger will be enormous; it will seem that all will be lost; at that moment, I will be with you; have confidence … the Cross will be treated with contempt; they will hurl it to the ground. Blood will flow; they will open up again the side of Our Lord. The streets will stream with blood …. the whole world will be in sadness."

Our Lady to St. Catherine Laboure
July 18, 1830

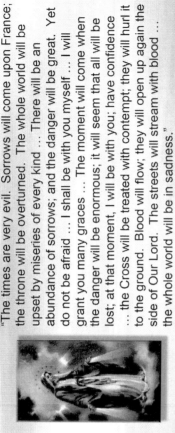

Source: Dirvin, J., "Saint Catherine Laboure of the Miraculous Medal," Tan Books and Publishers, 1984.

The Apparition of Our Lady at Lourdes

- Our Lady makes 18 apparitions to Bernadette Soubirous between February 11-July 16, 1858.
- Feb 18th – "I do not promise to make you happy in this world but in the other."
- Feb 24th – Penance, penance, penance! Pray to God for the conversion of sinners. Go and kiss the ground as a penance for sinners."
- Feb 25th – the Spring of Lourdes is revealed: "Go and drink at the spring and wash yourself in it."
- Mar 2nd – "Go and tell the priests that people are to come here in procession and to build a chapel here."
- Mar 25th – "I am the Immaculate Conception."

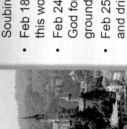

Source: Laurentin, R., "Bernadette of Lourdes," Darton, Longman and Todd, Ltd., 1999.
Sanctuary of Our Lady of Lourdes website: www.en.lourdes-france.org

---

To live this simple reality is to be caught up into an epic battle that spans heaven and earth.

The Miraculous Medal Apparition

- "Come to the foot of the altar. There graces will be shed upon all, great and little, who ask for them" (July 18, 1830).
- "[Mary's] arms swept wide in a gesture of motherly compassion, while from her jeweled fingers the rays of light streamed upon the white globe at her feet. An oval formed around the Blessed Virgin: 'O Mary, conceived without sin, pray for us who have recourse to thee.' Have a medal struck after this model. All who wear it will receive great graces. They should wear it around the neck. Graces will abound for persons who wear it with confidence" (November 27 , 1830).

Source: Dirvin, J., "Saint Catherine Laboure of the Miraculous Medal," Tan Books and Publishers, 1984.

Grace Flowing through the Family

- "Mary makes Bernadette enter into the particularly special atmosphere of the family ... Mary makes the Christians take the road to the Holy Family, where the Gospel is lived in its plentitude" (Fr. Andrew Doze).
- "There was issuing from below the threshold of the temple toward the east ... And wherever the river goes every living creature which swarms will live ... for this water goes there, that the waters of the sea may become fresh ... And on the banks, on both sides of the river, there will grow all kinds of trees for food. Their leaves will not wither nor their fruit fail ... their fruit will be for food, and their leaves for healing" (Ezekiel 47:1-12).

Source: Laurentin, R., "Bernadette of Lourdes," Darton, Longman and Todd, Ltd, 1990.
Laurentin, R., "Catherine Labouré: Visonary of the Miraculous Medal," Pauline Books and Media, 2006.
Doze, Fr. Andrew. "Saint Joseph: The Shadow of the Father." Trans. Audett, F. Alba House, 1992.

The Hidden Mystery of the Holy Family

- St. Catherine Labouré stated that the apparitions of Our Lady at Lourdes were intended for Rue du Bac.
- They make up a "single" revelation from God through Our Lady.
- When St. Catherine's mother died, she took down Our Lady's image ... her mother: "She took down Our Lady's image ... Throwing her arms about the statue ... 'Now, dear Blessed Mother ... now you will be my Mother!'"
- When St. Bernadette's father died, she took St. Joseph as her father: "Be very good. I will go and visit my father ... Don't you know that now my father is St. Joseph?"
- The Holy Family is hidden in these two great revelations.

Source: Laurentin, R., "Catherine Labouré – Visionary of the Miraculous Medal," Pauline Books and Media, 2006.
Dirvin, J., "St. Catherine Labouré of the Miraculous Medal, Tan Books and Publishers, Rockford, IL, 1994, pp. 15-16
Doze, Fr. Andrew. "Saint Joseph: The Shadow of the Father." Trans. Audett, F. Alba House, New York, 1992, p. 67

The Vision of the Holy Family

- "'Continue always to pray the Rosary every day' ... Then, opening her hands, she made them reflect on the sun, and as she ascended, the reflection of her own light continued to be projected on the sun itself ... After Our Lady had disappeared into the immense distance of the firmament, we beheld St. Joseph with the Child Jesus and Our Lady robed in white with a blue mantle, beside the sun. St. Joseph and the Child Jesus appeared to bless the world, for they traced the Sign of the Cross with their hands" (October 13, 1917).
- "I shall come to ask for the consecration of Russia to my Immaculate Heart, and the Communion of reparation on the First Saturdays" (July 13, 1917).

Source: "Fatima in Lucia's own Words," edited by Fr. Louis Kondor, SVD, The Ravengate Press, 1989, pp. 169-170 and 104

The Apparition of Our Lady at Fatima

- Our Lady appears to three peasant children six times between May 13 – October 13, 1917.
- "You have seen hell where the souls of poor sinners go. To save them, God wishes to establish in the world devotion to my Immaculate Heart ... When you see a night illumined by an unknown light, know that this is the great sign given you by God that He is about to punish the world for its crimes, by means of war, famine, and persecutions of the Church and of the Holy Father ... Russia will spread her errors throughout the world, causing wars and persecutions of the Church. The good will be martyred; the Holy Father will have much to suffer; various nations will be annihilated."

Source: "Fatima in Lucia's own Words," edited by Fr. Louis Kondor, SVD, The Ravengate Press, 1989, pp. 104-105.

Builders of a Civilization of Love

"The aspiration that humanity nurtures, amid countless injustices and sufferings, is the hope of a new civilization marked by freedom and peace. But for such an undertaking, a new generation of builders is needed ... You are the men and women of tomorrow. The future is in your hearts and in your hands. God is entrusting to you the task, at once difficult and uplifting, of working with him in the building of the civilization of love."

Pope John Paul II
Evening Vigil with Young People, #4
World Youth Day, Toronto, 2002
Downsview Park, Saturday 27, 200

The goal of our Lenten Journey this year is to journey to Nazareth so that we may listen to God's voice and "do whatever he tells us."

Everyone is called to enter into the mystery of Nazareth and be transformed. It is the universal call to holiness.

Have you received a call within a call?

Apostles to the Family

"It is especially necessary to recognize the unique place that ... belongs to the mission of married couples and Christian families, by virtue of the grace received in the sacrament. This mission must be placed at the service of the building up of the Church, the establishing of the Kingdom of God in history. This is demanded as an act of docile obedience to Christ the Lord. For it is He who, by virtue of the fact that marriage of baptized persons has been raised to a sacrament, confers upon Christian married couples a special mission as apostle, sending them as workers into His vineyard, and, in a very special way, into this field of the family."

Pope John Paul II
Familiaris Consortio, #71

St. Joseph at Nazareth

1. Divine Dialogue
2. Our Lady
3. Silence
4. Obedience to God's Representatives
5. Fidelity to State-in-Life
6. External Signs
7. Peace

Create Nazareth within our hearts.

Evaluate Dialogue with God

The Spirit of Nazareth Lenten Journey

- Identifies the seven steps in personal spiritual discernment according to the life of St. Joseph.
- Helps men enter into a personal dialogue with Jesus Christ.
- Helps men evaluate their dialogue with Jesus Christ to determine Christ's will in their life.
- Helps men embrace the particular will of God for their lives.

The Forty Days of Lent

- Days from Ash Wednesday to Holy Saturday.
- Does NOT include Sundays – the day of the Lord's Resurrection.
- Ash Wednesday and Good Friday are days of fast (1 meal plus two snacks) and abstinence (no meat).
- Fridays are days of abstinence (no meat).
- All days (except Sunday) are days of penance.

February 2016

Sun	Mon	Tue	Wed	Thu	Fri	Sat
7	8	9	10	11	12	13
14	15	16	17	18	19	20
21	22	23	24	25	26	27
28	29	1	2	3	4	5

March 2016

Sun	Mon	Tue	Wed	Thu	Fri	Sat
6	7	8	9	10	11	12
13	14	15	16	17	18	19
20	21	22	23	24	25	26
27	28	29	30	31	1	2

The Weeks of Lent

- Forty days of Lent are spread across 6 ½ weeks.
- Week of Ash Wednesday (½ week).
- First week of Lent; Second week of Lent; Third week of Lent; Fourth week of Lent; Fifth week of Lent.
- Holy Week
- Simple recommendation each week to help reinforce Principles of Discernment.

The Daily Lenten Program

1. Begin the day with a consecration of the day and ourselves to Our Lady.
2. Daily Lectio Divina using Scriptural passages and meditation starters.
3. Recitation of the Most Holy Rosary of the Blessed Virgin Mary.
4. Brief examination of conscience at the end of the day.

Small Group Discussion

Starter Questions

1. How can you be better informed about the spiritual reality of our day?
2. When are you going to set aside time to do you Lenten practices, especially the Rosary?

Next Week
A Divine Dialogue

Our goal is Lent is profound:

Encounter God.

Listen to his voice.

Do whatever he tells us.

SESSION 17
A Dialogue with God

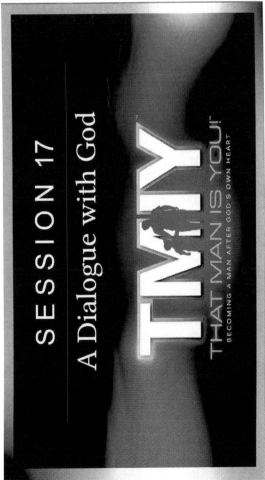

We have set for ourselves a lofty goal this Lenten season. Create Nazareth in our hearts so that we may hear and fulfill God's will in our life.

Entry into the Spirit of Nazareth

- "O Mary Immaculate, O glorious Joseph! And you, St. John, beloved disciple of the Divine Heart, teach me the great science of love" (St. Bernadette).

- "The Church must make this journey which takes her from the temple she has built for herself to this house that God makes for her ... that is, to true interior life, the life of the Holy Family ... Mary makes Christians take the road to the Holy Family, where the Gospel is lived in its plenitude" (Fr. Andrew Doze).

Source: Doze, Fr. Andrew, "Saint Joseph: The Shadow of the Father," Trans. Anslett, F., Alba House, New York, 1992, p. 68 and pp. 72-73.

The Daily Lenten Program

1. Begin the day with a consecration of the day and ourselves to Our Lady.

2. Daily Lectio Divina using Scriptural passages and meditation starters.

3. Recitation of the Most Holy Rosary of the Blessed Virgin Mary.

4. Brief examination of conscience at the end of the day.

The Weekly Lenten Program

1. Discernment at Nazareth
   - Enter into a substantial dialogue with God.
2. Practical Recommendation
   - Put down all your external prayer guides.
   - Get in front of the Eucharist or your favorite image of Christ.
   - In your own words, tell him everything that is happening in your life – particularly the things that are causing your anxiety.
   - Ask God to help you.

St. Joseph at Nazareth

1. Divine Dialogue
2. Our Lady
3. Silence — } Create Nazareth within our hearts.
4. Obedience to God's Representatives
5. Fidelity to State-in-Life
6. External Signs — } Discern the movement of the Holy Spirit in our hearts.
7. Peace

St. Joseph and the Primacy of Prayer

"When his mother Mary had been betrothed to Joseph, before they came together she was found to be with child of the Holy Spirit; and her husband Joseph, being a just man and unwilling to put her to shame, resolved to send her away quietly. But as he considered this, behold, an angel of the Lord appeared to him in a dream, saying, 'Joseph, son of David, do not fear to take Mary your wife, for that which is conceived in her is of the Holy Spirit; she will bear a son, and you shall call his name Jesus' … When Joseph woke from sleep, he did as the angel of the Lord commanded him."

Matthew 1:18-25

If we wish to discover and fulfill God's will in our life, we must enter into Nazareth and learn from St. Joseph his great art of prayer.

The Temple at Nazareth

- "Jesus went down with them and came to Nazareth, and was obedient to them ... And Jesus increased in wisdom and in stature, and in favor with God and man" (Luke 2:52).
- "Samuel continued to grow both in stature and in favor with the Lord and with men" (1 Samuel 2:26).
- "The secrets Mary had been in charge of revealing to Jesus, secrets wrapped in silence and darkness. Instead of opposing the one he called 'my Father' against the carpenter of Nazareth, Jesus, on the threshold of his conscious adolescence, had to see them both together in the same glance" (Fr. Andrew Doze).

Source: Doze, Fr. Andrew, "Saint Joseph: The Shadow of the Father," Trans. Audet, F., Alba House, New York, 1992, p. 67.

The Lessons of St. Joseph

"Especially persons of prayer should always be attached to [St. Joseph] ... Those who cannot find a master to reach them prayer should take this glorious saint for their master, and they will not go astray."

St. Theresa of Avila

Source: St. Theresa of Avila, Collected Works, v. 1, Trans. Kavanaugh, K., et al., ICS Publications, Washington, D.C., 1976, The Book of Her Life, pp. 86-91.

Jesus in the Temple as a Child

"Now his parents went to Jerusalem every year at the feast of Passover. And when he was twelve years old ... and when the feast was ended ... the boy Jesus stayed behind in Jerusalem ... supposing him to be in the company they went a day's journey ... and when they did not find him, they returned to Jerusalem, seeking him. After three days they found him in the temple ... and his mother said to him, 'Son, why have you treated us so? Behold, your father and I have been looking for you anxiously.' And he said to them ... 'Did you not know that I must be in my Fathers house?'"

Luke 2:41-51

Jesus returns to the Temple as an Adult

"Jesus entered the temple of God and drove out all who sold and bought in the temple, and he overturned the tables of the money-changers and the seats of those who sold pigeons. He said to them, 'It is written, 'My house shall be called a house of prayer'; but you make it a den of robbers.'"

Matthew 21:12-13

St. Theresa of Avila took St. Joseph as her patron and she became "the doctor of prayer" in the Catholic Church. She helps us to understand the stages of prayer.

Source: St. Teresa of Avila, Collected Works, v.1, 2nd Edition. "The Book of her Life." Trans. Kavanaugh, K., et al, ICS Publications, Washington, 1987.

The Pathway of Prayer: Vocal Prayer

- Entry state in the prayer life. Characterized by much activity and the soul actively seeking God.
- Audible prayers – frequently from memory.
- "Because it is external and so thoroughly human, vocal prayer is the form of prayer most readily accessible to groups" (Catechism #2704).
- "If while speaking I thoroughly understand and know that I am speaking with God and I have greater awareness of this than I do of the words I'm saying, mental and vocal prayer are joined" (St. Teresa of Avila, The Way of Perfection, #22).

Source: St. Teresa of Avila, Collected Works, v.2. "The Way of Perfection," Trans. Kavanaugh, K., et al, ICS Publications, Washington, 1980.

The Pathway of Prayer: Meditation

- "Meditation is above all a quest. The mind seeks to understand the why and how of the Christian life, in order to adhere and respond to what the Lord is asking. The required attentiveness is difficult to sustain. We are usually helped by books" (Catechism #2705).
- "With a book I began to collect [my wandering thoughts], and my soul was drawn to recollection. And many times just opening the book was enough; at other times I read a little, and at others a great deal, according to the favor the Lord granted me" (St. Teresa of Avila, The Book of her Life, #4).

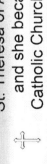

Source: St. Teresa of Avila, Collected Works, v.1. "The Book of her Life." Trans. Kavanaugh, K., et al, ICS Publications, Washington, 1987.

The Pathway of Prayer: Prayer of Simplicity

- Acquired contemplative state entered through the soul's own efforts.
- "This prayer is called 'recollection' because the soul collects its faculties together and enters within itself to be with God" (St. Teresa of Avila, The Way of Perfection, #28).
- "Those who by such a method can enclose themselves within this little heaven of our soul, where the Maker of heaven and earth is present … they are following an excellent path and that they will not fail to drink water from the fount" (St. Teresa of Avila, The Way of Perfection, #28).

Source: St. Teresa of Avila, Collected Works, v.2. "The Way of Perfection," Trans. Kavanaugh, K., et al, ICS Publications, Washington, 1980.

The Pathway of Prayer: Prayer of Quiet

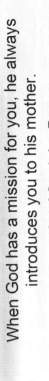

- The soul is totally captivated by divine love and enjoys repose in God.
- "This prayer is something supernatural, something we cannot procure through our own efforts" (St. Teresa of Avila, The Way of Perfection, #31).
- "God begins now to give us His kingdom here below … In it the soul enters into peace or, better, the Lord puts it at peace by His presence … The state resembles an interior and exterior swoon; for the exterior man … doesn't want any activity. But like one who has almost reached the end of his journey … he wants to rest so as to be better able to continue" (St. Teresa of Avila, The Way of Perfection, #31).

Source: St. Teresa of Avila, Collected Works, v.2, "The Way of Perfection," Trans. Kavanaugh, K. et al. ICS Publications, Washington. 1980.

When God has a mission for you, he always introduces you to his mother.

The Life of St. John Bosco

The Mission of St. John Bosco

Don Bosco dreamed that he was "in a field surrounded by a crowd of boys. Some … were fighting and using bad language. On hearing the language he lost his temper, dashed in among them and laid about him with his fists … and a battle royal began … In the middle of this ruckus appeared a noble-looking Man … 'Come here,' he said … 'You will never help these boys by beating them. Be kind to them, lead them, teach them that sin is evil and that purity is a precious gift.' … 'Who are you to tell me to do all these difficult things?' Don Bosco demanded. 'I am the Son of the woman your mother taught you to salute three times a day … By listening to the woman I shall send to you, you will do everything with ease.' The Man disappeared and the boys at once changed into dogs, wolves and other wild animals. Trembling with fear, he turned to find a beautiful and gracious Lady at his side. 'Don't be afraid,' she said … 'What I shall do for these animals, you must do for all my children' … When she had finished speaking, he saw that the wild animals had indeed been changed to lambs … Confused by what he saw, he started to cry, 'I don't understand!' 'Do not worry, my child,' the Lady comforted him. 'You will understand everything in good time.'"

Source: Lappin, P., Give Me Souls: Life of Don Bosco, Salesiana Publishers, New York, 1986. "The Lady and the Dream, passim to Chapter 1

Mary would like to help you enter more deeply into the mysteries of our faith.

The perfect means is the Rosary. Through it we discover Mary's contemplation of the divine mysteries.

Our first step to enter into Nazareth so that we can discern and fulfill God's will is to become men of prayer.

Take St. Joseph for your guide.

A Practical Recommendation

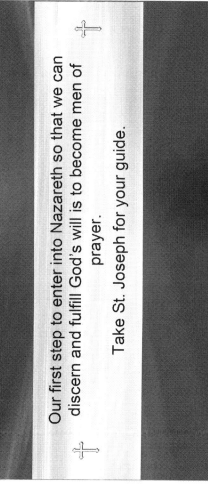

- Pray your Rosary while walking outdoors or in nature.
- Research indicates that the Rosary is one of the most effective means of prayer.
- Time in nature lowers stress.
- Walking increases blood flow, but not so much that your main focus is exercising.
- "The most important reason for strongly encouraging the practice of the Rosary is that it represents a most effective means of fostering among the faithful that commitment to the contemplation of the Christian mystery" (St. Pope John Paul II, Rosarium Virginis Mariae, #5).

Source: Anstasi, M., "A Preliminary Study of the Acute Effects of Religious Ritual on Anxiety," The Journal of Alternative and Complementary Medicine. V. 14, No. 2, 2008, pp. 163-165.

Small Group Discussion

Starter Questions

1. What does your normal daily prayer look like?
2. What things do you need to minimize so that you can dedicate more time to your prayer life?

Next Week
Receiving the Gift of Mary

SESSION 18

Receiving the Gift of Mary

TMIY

THAT MAN IS YOU!

BECOMING A MAN AFTER GOD'S OWN HEART

☩ We have set for ourselves a lofty goal this Lenten season. Create Nazareth in our hearts so that we may hear and fulfill God's will in our life.

☩

Entry into the Spirit of Nazareth

- "O Mary Immaculate, O glorious Joseph! And you, St. John, beloved disciple of the Divine Heart, teach me the great science of love" (St. Bernadette).

- "The Church must make this journey which takes her from the temple she has built for herself to this house that God makes for her ... that is, to true interior life, the life of the Holy Family .... Mary makes Christians take the road to the Holy Family, where the Gospel is lived in its plenitude" (Fr. Andrew Doze).

Source: Doze, Fr. Andrew, "Saint Joseph: The Shadow of the Father," Trans. Andert, F., Alba House, New York, 1992, p. 68 nad pp. 72-73.

The Daily Lenten Program

The Spirit of Nazareth

A Layman's Journey to Fatherhood

BY STEVE BOLLMAN

1. Begin the day with a consecration of the day and ourselves to Our Lady.

2. Daily Lectio Divina using Scriptural passages and meditation starters.

3. Recitation of the Most Holy Rosary of the Blessed Virgin Mary.

4. Brief examination of conscience at the end of the day.

The Weekly Lenten Program

1. Discernment at Nazareth
   - Bring Mary into your spiritual life in a more profound way
2. Practical Recommendation
   - Ask Christ to help you love his mother as he did.
   - Wear the Miraculous Medal around your neck every day.
   - Begin each day by consecrating it to Our Lady.
   - Say 5 decades of the Rosary every day.

Receiving the Gift of Mary

"When his mother Mary had been betrothed to Joseph, before they came together she was found to be with child of the Holy Spirit … as Joseph considered this, behold, an angel of the Lord appeared to him in a dream, saying, 'Joseph, son of David, do not fear to take Mary your wife' … When Joseph woke from sleep, he did as the angel of the Lord commanded him; he took his wife."

Matthew 1:18-25

St. Joseph at Nazareth

1. Divine Dialogue
2. Our Lady
3. Silence
4. Obedience to God's Representatives

} Create Nazareth within our hearts.

5. Fidelity to State-in-Life
6. External Signs
7. Peace

} Discern the movement of the Holy Spirit in our hearts.

✞ In a very profound way, Nazareth was born when St. Joseph received Mary into his home.

We must allow St. Joseph to help us bring Mary into the Nazareth of our hearts. ✞

The Gift of Mary

"Standing by the cross of Jesus were his mother, and his mother's sister, Mary the wife of Clopas, and Mary Magdalene. When Jesus saw his mother and the disciple whom he loved standing near, he said to his mother, 'Woman, behold your son!' Then he said to the disciple, 'Behold, your mother!' And from that hour the disciple took her to his own home."

John 19:25-27

Our Spiritual Mother

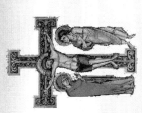

"The man at the foot of the Cross is John, 'the disciple whom he loved.' But it is not he alone. Following tradition, the Council does not hesitate to call Mary 'the Mother of Christ and mother of mankind' ... Indeed she is 'clearly the mother of the members of Christ.'"

Pope John Paul II
Redemptoris Mater, #23

As our spiritual mother, Mary is working to give birth to Christ in us. We must strive to help her in this labor.

A Divine Motherhood

"The words uttered by Jesus from the Cross signify that the motherhood of her who bore Christ finds a 'new' continuation in the Church and through the Church, symbolized and represented by John ... Mary's 'motherhood' of the Church is the reflection and extension of her motherhood of the Son of God."

Pope John Paul II
Redemptoris Mater, #24

The Sons of God

- "See what love the Father has given us, that we should be called children of God; and so we are" (1 John 3:1-2).

- "It is no longer I who live, but Christ who lives in me … I live by faith in the Son of God, who loved me and gave himself for me" (Galatians 2:20).

Sons of God – Sons of Mary

- "For by His incarnation the Son of God has united Himself in some fashion with every man" (Gaudium et Spes, #22).

- "Therefore all we who are united to Christ … have issued from the womb of Mary like a body united to its head … in a spiritual and mystical fashion, we are all children of Mary" (Pope St. Pius X, Ad Diem Illum Laetissimum, #10).

Learning the Obedience of Christ

- "There was a marriage in Cana of Galilee … When the wine failed, the mother of Jesus said to him, 'They have no wine.' And Jesus said to her, 'Woman, what have you to do with me? My hour has not yet come.' His mother said to the servants, 'Do whatever he tells you' … Jesus said to them, 'Fill the [six] jars with water and draw some out, and take to the steward of the feast' … the steward said, 'You have kept the good wine until now.'"

John 2:1-11

Fulfilling the Will of God

- "For I have come down from heaven, not to do my own will, but the will of him who sent me" (John 6:36).

- "For God so loved the world that he gave his only Son, that whoever believes in him should not perish but have eternal life" (John 3:16).

- With and in Christ we are to offer ourselves in sacrifice to manifest the Father "who is rich in mercy" (Ephesians 2:4).

Mary as the Ladder to God

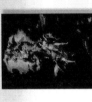

- "Jacob came to a certain place, and stayed there that night … and he dreamed that there was a ladder set up on the earth, and the top of it reached to heaven: and behold, the angels of God were ascending and descending on it" (Genesis 28:10-12).
- "The lowliness of Mary was made the heavenly ladder, by which God descended upon earth" (St. Augustine).
- "The Most High God came down to us in a perfect way through the humble Virgin Mary, without losing anything of his divinity or holiness. It is likewise through Mary that we poor creatures must ascend to almighty God in a perfect manner" (St. Louis de Montfort).

Source: St. Augustine. Commentary on the Gospel of St. Luke. Catena Aurea, v III Part I, Preserving Christian Publications, Inc. Albany, NY, 1995, p. 44
St. Louis de Montfort, True Devotion to Mary, #157, taken from God Alone: The Collected Writings of St. Louis Marie de Montfort, Montfort Publications, Bayshore, NY, 1987, p. 338.

John Paul II and the Consecration to Mary

"Therefore, O Mother, like the Apostle John, we wish to take you into our home, that we may learn from you to become like your Son. 'Woman, behold your Son.' Here we stand before you to entrust to your maternal care ourselves, the Church, the entire world … grant that … the darkness will not prevail over the light. To you, Dawn of Salvation, we commit our journey through the new Millennium, so that with you as guide all people may know Christ, the light of the world and its only Savior."

St. Pope John Paul II
October 8, 2000

If we wish to more profoundly live our Christian lives, then we must enter into greater union with Mary.

The Church has looked forward to this period for centuries.

Source: St. Louis de Montfort, "True Devotion to Mary," taken from God Alone: The Collected Writings of St. Louis Marie de Montfort, Montfort Publications, Bayshore, NY, 1987, p. 303 and pp. 306-307.

Mary and Apostles of a New Springtime

- "As Mary was the way by which Jesus first came to us, she will again be the way by which he will come to us the second time though not in the same manner" (St. Louis de Montfort, True Devotion to Mary, #50.4).
- "They will be true apostles … They will carry the crucifix in their right hand and the rosary in their left, and the holy names of Jesus and Mary on their heart. The simplicity and self-sacrifice of Jesus will be reflected in their whole behavior. Such are the great men who are to come" (St. Louis de Montfort, True Devotion to Mary, ##58-59).

Practical Recommendations

- Wear the Miraculous Medal around your neck.
- Begin each day by consecrating it to Mary and asking her to guide you.
- Say the Rosary everyday.
- Make the St. Louis de Montfort "Total Consecration to Mary."
- Have a statue or image of Our Lady in a prominent place in your home.

✝

Mary is very important in our times. We must enter into closer union with her.

✝

Small Group Discussion

Starter Questions

1. What role does Mary currently serve in your spiritual life?
2. How are you going to help make a home for Mary – in your heart and in your spiritual life?

Next Week
Enter into Great Silence

SESSION 19

Enter into Great Silence

TMIY

THAT MAN IS YOU!

BECOMING A MAN AFTER GOD'S OWN HEART

We have set for ourselves a lofty goal this Lenten season. Create Nazareth in our hearts so that we may hear and fulfill God's will in our life.

Entry into the Spirit of Nazareth

- "O Mary Immaculate, O glorious Joseph! And you, St. John, beloved disciple of the Divine Heart, teach me the great science of love" (St. Bernadette).

- "The Church must make this journey which takes her from the temple she has built for herself to this house that God makes for her … that is, to true interior life, the life of the Holy Family … Mary makes Christians take the road to the "Holy Family, where the Gospel is lived in its plenitude" (Fr. Andrew Doze).

Source: Doze, Fr. Andrew. "Saint Joseph: The Shadow of the Father," Trans. Audett, F., Alba House, New York, 1992, p. 68 and pp. 72-73.

The Daily Lenten Program

1. Begin the day with a consecration of the day and ourselves to Our Lady.

2. Daily Lectio Divina using Scriptural passages and meditation starters.

3. Recitation of the Most Holy Rosary of the Blessed Virgin Mary.

4. Brief examination of conscience at the end of the day.

The Weekly Lenten Program

1. Discernment at Nazareth
   - Enter into profound silence in the presence of the Lord.
2. Practical Recommendation
   - Establish a dedicated prayer place in your home.
   - Place an image of Christ that resonates to you personally in this place.
   - Begin and end the day with 10-15 minutes of silence in this place of prayer.
   - Establish time to "come away" with Christ.

St. Joseph at Nazareth

1. Divine Dialogue
2. Our Lady
3. Silence   } Create Nazareth within our hearts.
4. Obedience to God's Representatives
5. Fidelity to State-in-Life } Discern the movement of the Holy Spirit in our hearts.
6. External Signs
7. Peace

The Silence of St. Joseph

- Does not speak a single word in Scripture.
- Royal line, but is poor.
- Know nothing of past, parents, death.
- Amazingly absent from Church Fathers.
- No major church in Holy Land.
- No major church in Rome.
- 1129: 1st church in west (Bologna)
- 1479: Feast in Universal Church
- 1729: Name added to Litany of Saints.
- 1870: Patron of Universal Church.
- 1962: Name added to Roman Canon.

Now comes the tricky part!

We must learn St. Joseph's great lesson on silence – but he didn't tell us how!

He showed us!

The Silence of God

"For God alone my soul waits in silence, for my hope is from him. He only is my rock and my salvation, my fortress; I shall not be shaken. On God rests my deliverance and my honor; my mighty rock, my refuge is God. Trust in him at all times, O people; pour out your heart before him; God is a refuge for us."

Psalm 62:5-8

Developing Interior Silence

"And a great storm of wind arose, and the waves beat into the boat, so that the boat was already filling ... they woke Jesus and said to him, 'Teacher, do you not care if we perish?' And he awoke and rebuked the wind, and said to the sea, 'Peace! Be still!' And the wind ceased, and there was a great calm ... And they were filled with awe."

Mark 4:37-41

On a daily basis, we need to enter into silence to listen to the voice of God. A perfect means to accomplish this is the practice of Lectio Divina.

Finding Christ in the Scriptures

- "You search the Scriptures, because you think that in them you have eternal life; and it is they that bear witness to me" (John 5:39).

- "Let [the faithful] remember, however, that prayer should accompany the reading of Sacred Scripture, so that a dialogue takes place between God and man. For 'we speak to him when we pray; we listen to him when we read the divine oracles'" (Catechism #2653).

- There are four elements to Lectio Divina: Reading, Meditation, Prayer and Contemplation.

Meditatio or Meditation

- Dwelling at leisure on a morsel of text.
- Personalize passage: "What is God saying to ME through the passage?"
- Do not work hard to actively try to "crack" the text.
- Listen so that the text might speak.
- Let God speak through the text.

Contemplatio or Contemplation

- God comes to the soul.
- The soul experiences God's love being poured into it.
- This is God's initiative to be received by the soul as "gift."
- The soul is passive and receives or "lingers" as long as God's presence is experienced.

Lectio or Reading

- Place the Word of God on your lips.
- Gently read a passage from the Bible.
- When a thought, word or line strikes you, stop and dwell on that text, repeating it slowly over and over.
- When the passage has "dried up," move on to the next passage.

Oratio or Prayer

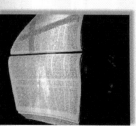

- The Word moves from the lips to the heart.
- Desire for the text to be "opened up."
- "Lord, that I might see!"
- It is personalized.
- It is ultimately desire for communion with God.

Time for Christ

"Jesus said to them, 'Come away by yourselves to a lonely place, and rest a while.' For many were coming and going, and they had no leisure even to eat. And they went away in the boat to a lonely place by themselves.

Mark 6:31-32

✝

God speaks through the Scriptures.

God speaks through the Magisterium.

God also speaks directly to our heart.

We must create the opportunity to hear him.

✝

Pilgrimage: Time with God

- Pilgrimage: Combines time with other people and the opportunity to see a place where heaven and earth have touched in a special way.
- Paradisus Dei leads pilgrimages to important sites:
  - Lourdes: Apparition site of Our Lady in 1858.
  - Rome: Seat of Pope, tombs of 7 Apostles, filled with spiritual treasures.
  - Holy Land: The land where Jesus Christ physically lived, died and rose from the dead.
- University of Notre Dame
  - Spiritual tie to Lourdes, Frances.
  - One of the most beautiful churches in U.S.
  - Grotto of Lourdes as spiritual heart of campus.

God Speaks in the Silence

"Kneeling here, before the grotto of Massabielle, I feel deeply that I have reached the goal of my pilgrimage. This cave, where Mary appeared, is the heart of Lourdes. It reminds us of the cave of Mount Horeb where Elijah met the Lord, who spoke to him in 'a still, small voice' (1 Kings 19:12) ... When the Virgin Mary appeared to Bernadette in the grotto of Massabielle, she began a dialogue between Heaven and earth ... Mary asked that people should come here in procession ... for more than a century the Christian people have faithfully responded to that maternal summons ... This year the Pope joins you in this act of devotion and love for the Most Holy Virgin, the glorious woman of the Book of Revelation, crowned with twelve stars (cf. Rev 12:1) ... Dear brothers and sisters! From this grotto of Massabielle the Blessed Virgin speaks to us too, the Christians of the third millennium. Let us listen to her."

Pope John Paul II

Pilgrimage to Lourdes, August 14-15, 2004

Creating Silence at Home

- The TMIY Don Bosco – Lourdes "12 Day Novena"
  - January 31 – February 11
  - Time to evaluate spiritual plan-of-life and/or apostolic activities.
- The TMIY Miraculous Medal – Immaculate Conception "12 Day Novena"
  - November 27 – December 8
  - Time to evaluate spiritual plan-of-life and/or apostolic activities.
- Weekly or Monthly gathering with TMIY men.

If we are willing to create silence in our lives, then we will be able to hear when God speaks in his "still, small voice."

A Practical Recommendation

- Have a dedicated place of prayer in your home or in nature.
- Have images of Christ that speak to you personally.
- Place yourself in God's presence.
- Have at least 5 minutes of silence.
- Read Scripture practicing Lectio Divina.
- Attend a Retreat or make a TMIY "12 Day Novena" each year.
- Attend a pilgrimage when possible.
- Get together with other TMIY men to work on your spiritual life.

Small Group Discussion

Starter Questions

1. What are the major obstacles for you having silence in your life? What are going to do about them?
2. When is the best time for you to have silence?

Next Week
Hearing the Voice of God

We have set for ourselves a lofty goal this Lenten season. Create Nazareth in our hearts so that we may hear and fulfill God's will in our life.

SESSION 20

Hearing the Voice of God

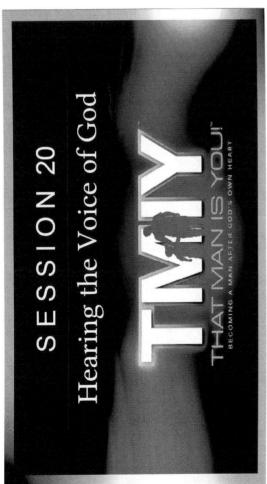

TMIY

THAT MAN IS YOU!

BECOMING A MAN AFTER GOD'S OWN HEART

The Daily Lenten Program

The Spirit of Nazareth

BY STEVE BOLLMAN

1. Begin the day with a consecration of the day and ourselves to Our Lady.

2. Daily Lectio Divina using Scriptural passages and meditation starters.

3. Recitation of the Most Holy Rosary of the Blessed Virgin Mary.

4. Brief examination of conscience at the end of the day.

Entry into the Spirit of Nazareth

- "O Mary Immaculate, O glorious Joseph! And you, St. John, beloved disciple of the Divine Heart, teach me the great science of love" (St. Bernadette).

- "The Church must make this journey which takes her from the temple she has built for herself to this house that God makes for her … that is, to true interior life, the life of the Holy Family … Mary makes Christians take the road to the Holy Family, where the Gospel is lived in its plenitude" (Fr. Andrew Doze).

Source: Doze, Fr. Andrew, "Saint Joseph: The Shadow of the Father," Trans Andrif, F. Alba House, New York, 1992, p. 68 and pp. 72-73.

The Weekly Lenten Program

1. Discernment at Nazareth
   - Obedience to God's representatives.
2. Practical Recommendation
   - Learn to be more aware of the interior movements of your soul.
   - Learn the very basic principles of discernment.
   - Develop a relationship with an external, objective third party who can help guide you.

St. Joseph at Nazareth

1. Divine Dialogue
2. Our Lady
3. Silence
4. Obedience to God's Representatives
5. Fidelity to State-in-Life
6. External Signs
7. Peace

Create Nazareth within our hearts.

Discern the movement of the Holy Spirit in our hearts.

The Desire of Joseph's Heart: Mercy

- "Before they came together Mary was found to be with child" (Matthew 1:18).
- "If there is a betrothed virgin, and a man meets her … and lies with her, then you shall … stone them to death" (Deuteronomy 2:23).
- In Judaism, a just man fulfills the Mosaic Law.
- St. Joseph was going to break the Law.
- Further, we was going to divorce Mary without telling anyone the reason.
- He was going to take Mary's "shame" as his own.
  - "Go and learn what this means, 'I desire mercy and not sacrifice'" (Matthew 9:13).

✝

Nazareth is above all a place where God can speak to our hearts. In this moment he will raise in our hearts holy desires. These desires will be in harmony with God's voice speaking through the hierarchy.

✝

The Obedience of St. Joseph

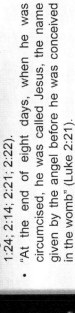

- "When Joseph woke from sleep, he did as the angel of the Lord commanded him" (Matthew 1:24; 2:14; 2:21; 2:22).
- "At the end of eight days, when he was circumcised, he was called Jesus, the name given by the angel before he was conceived in the womb" (Luke 2:21).
- When the time came for their purification according to the law of Moses, they brought him to the Lord as it is written in the law of the Lord" (Luke 2:22).
- "Now his parents went to Jerusalem every year at the feast of Passover" (Luke 2:41).

Confirmation by God

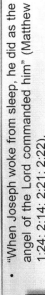

"When his mother Mary had been betrothed to Joseph, before they came together she was found to be with child of the Holy Spirit ... as Joseph considered this, behold, an angel of the Lord appeared to him in a dream, saying, 'Joseph, son of David, do not fear to take Mary your wife' ... When Joseph woke from sleep, he did as the angel of the Lord commanded him; he took his wife."

Matthew 1:18-25

Holy Desires in the Heart

"As a hart longs for flowing streams, so longs my soul for thee, O God. My soul thirsts for God, for the living God ... These things I remember, as I pour out my soul: how I went with the throng, and led them in procession to the house of God, with glad shouts and songs of thanksgiving, a multitude keeping festival ... Hope in God; for I shall again praise him, my help and my God."

Psalm 42:1-6

God will also speak to our hearts. He will raise in them holy desires. We must learn to discern these desires and have them obedient to the voice of God speaking through the Church.

Extraordinary Signs

- Sensible or corporal visions: A person sees with their eyes Christ, Our Lady or the saints.
- Imaginary visions: A person sees Christ, Our Lady or the saints not with the eyes, but in the mind with the imagination. Could be a dream.
- Intellectual visions: A person does not have a sensible image, but knows (i.e. "sees") that Christ, Our Lady or the saints are present.
- Auricular supernatural word: A person hears with their ears words from God, Christ, Our Lady or the saints.
- Imaginary supernatural words: A person hears words from God, Christ, Our Lady or the saints not with the ears, but in the mind heart.
- Intellectual supernatural words: A person does not hear a sensible word with the ear or imagination, but perceives in the intellect a word spoken by God, Christ, Our Lady or the saints.

Source: Garrigou-Lagrange, R., "The Three Ages of the Interior Life," v. 2, Tau Books and Publishers, Rockford, IL, 1989, pp. 589-592

The Magisterium: The Voice of God

- "On the evening of that day, the first day of the week ... Jesus came and stood among them and said to them ... 'Peace be with you. As the Father has sent me, even so I send you.' And when he had said this, he breathed on them, and said to them, 'Receive the Holy Spirit'" (John 20:19-23).

- "He who hears you hears me, and he who rejects you rejects me" (Luke 10:16).

Discernment of Ordinary Movements

- Current spiritual state.
- The manner in which the movement is perceived: "The good angel touches souls ... sweetly, lightly, gently, just as when a drop of water penetrates a sponge. The bad angel touches them in a stinging way ... with noise and agitation: just as when a drop of water splashes on a stone" (St. Ignatius of Loyola).
- Timing: "A spiritual person ... ought to consider it observantly and distinguish attentively between the time of consolation and the time following" (St. Ignatius of Loyola).

Source: Ronca, A., "A Do It At Home Retreat," Ignatius Press, San Francisco, CA, 1991, pp. 221-226.

We must discern our holy desires relative to the voice of God speaking through the Magisterium.

Today they are giving us a message that relates to the family.

The Life of Nazareth

Holy Family at Nazareth

1. The Niddah Laws on sexual purity (Cf. Leviticus 15:19ff).
2. The separation of the Challah (Cf. Numbers 15:20).
3. The Nerot Laws (Exodus 20:8).
4. The angel is sent to Mary and Joseph to open their minds.
5. Mary finds God in self.
6. Joseph finds God in Mary.
7. The Christian home is born of mercy.

Paradisus Dei

1. Honor your wedding vows.
2. Use money for others.
3. Give God some of your time.
4. Set your mind on the things above.
5. Find God in yourself.
6. Find God in other people.
7. Make it easy to be good and hard to be bad.

The "School" of the Home at Nazareth

"Nazareth is a kind of school where we may begin to discover what Christ's life was like and even to understand his Gospel ... Here everything speaks to us, everything has meaning ... How I would like to return to my childhood and attend the simple yet profound school that is Nazareth!"

Blessed Pope Paul VI,
Address at the Basilica of the Annunciation
January 5, 1964

The Future of the World and Church

- Impact on the Person
  - Twice as likely to be "very happy" with life.
  - Better health – almost 2 weeks fewer sick days per year.
  - Accumulate 4 times the pre-retirement wealth.
- Impact on the Church
  - Approximately 70% more likely to attend Church almost weekly or more often.
  - Large intact family is the source of vocations.
- Impact on Larger Society
  - Reduces the probability that a child will be incarcerated for a crime by one-half.
  - Reduces the probability of childhood poverty by one-half.
  - Reduces the probability of being an unwed mother by two-thirds.

Source: General Social Survey, 1972-2012.
Wilcox, J., and Koso, G., "Does Marital History Matter? Marital Status and Wealth Outcomes Among Preretirement Adults", 2002.
CARA, "The Class of 2014: Survey of Ordinands to the Priesthood," April 2014
Waite, L., et al., "The Case for Marriage," Broadway Books, New York, 2000.

Seven Steps to a Superabundant Marriage

Percentage Ever Divorced

	Doesn't Pray	No Degree	Attend <1/yr	Stray	Cohabit	Base	No Cohabit	No Stray	Attend Almost Wkly	Bachelor Degree	Pray Daily
	100.0	100.0	59.3	57.8	38.4	28.5	12.1	11.0	9.0	3.1	0.0

Source: General Social Survey, 1972-2012.

Practical Recommendations

- Ask God to help you understand how he wishes to use you – for your own family and for others.
- Become more aware of the spiritual movements within your heart.
- Learn the basic principles of spiritual discernment.
- Establish a relationship with a trusted third party who can help you discern.
- Regularly read the statements of the Pope – best source is www.vatican.va

---

The family is the foundation of society. A small change for the better has profound ramifications for the individual, the Church and larger society.

Small Group Discussion

Starter Questions

1. What holy desires are in your heart for the glory of God and the good of souls?
2. Who can you use as your trusted third party spiritual mentor?

Next Week
Fidelity to your State-in-Life

SESSION 21

Fidelity to your State-in-Life

TMIY

THAT MAN IS YOU!

BECOMING A MAN AFTER GOD'S OWN HEART

Lent is speeding to its conclusion. Our goal: Create Nazareth in our hearts so that we may hear and fulfill God's will in our life.

Entry into the Spirit of Nazareth

- "O Mary Immaculate, O glorious Joseph! And you, St. John, beloved disciple of the Divine Heart, teach me the great science of love" (St. Bernadette).

- "The Church must make this journey which takes her from the temple she has built for herself to this house that God makes for her ... that is, to true interior life, the life of the Holy Family ... Mary makes Christians take the road to the Holy Family, where the Gospel is lived in its plenitude" (Fr. Andrew Doze).

Source: Doze, Fr. Andrew. "Saint Joseph: The Shadow of the Father," Trans. Anselm P., Alba House, New York, 1992, p. 68 and pp. 72-73.

The Daily Lenten Program

1. Begin the day with a consecration of the day and ourselves to Our Lady.

2. Daily Lectio Divina using Scriptural passages and meditation starters.

3. Recitation of the Most Holy Rosary of the Blessed Virgin Mary.

4. Brief examination of conscience at the end of the day.

The Weekly Lenten Program

1. Discernment at Nazareth
   - Fidelity to State-in-Life.
2. Practical Recommendation
   - Pray for the grace to live your life as husband and father as your pathway to holiness.
   - Use the everyday things of family life to offer as sacrifices to God.
   - Use the everyday things of family life to make acts of charity to your family members.

St. Joseph at Nazareth

1. Divine Dialogue — Create Nazareth within our hearts.
2. Our Lady
3. Silence
4. Obedience to God's Representatives
5. Fidelity to State-in-Life — Discern the movement of the Holy Spirit in our hearts.
6. External Signs
7. Peace

The Importance of the Holy Family

"In this great undertaking, which is the renewal of all things in Christ, marriage … becomes a new reality … We see that at the beginning of the New Testament, as at the beginning of the Old, there is a married couple. But whereas Adam and Eve were the source of evil which was unleashed on the world, Joseph and Mary are the summit from which holiness spreads over all the earth."

St. Pope John Paul II
Redemptoris Custos, #7

There are two simple realities that we need to grasp.

The greatest saint in heaven is a wife and mother.

The second greatest saint in heaven is a husband and father.

The Immaculate Conception of Mary

"She was entirely a fit habitation for Christ, not because of the state of her body, but because of her original grace ... The most Blessed Virgin Mary was, from the first moment of her conception, by a singular grace and privilege of almighty God and by virtue of the merits of Jesus Christ, Savior of the human race, preserved immune from all stain of original sin."

Blessed Pope Pius IX
Ineffabilis Deus, 1854

The Holiness of the Holy Family

- "This is a consequence of the hypostatic union: humanity taken up into the unity of the Divine Person of the Word-Son, Jesus Christ. Together with human nature, all that is human, and especially the family – as the first dimension of man's existence in the world – is also taken up in Christ" (St. Pope John Paul II, *Redemptoris Custos*, #21).

- The Holy Family belongs to "the order of the hypostatic union."

This is the model of your family. Christ is present in your spouse and children. You have the unfathomable dignity to help him attain to full stature.

The Holiness of St. Joseph

"The admirable St. Joseph was given to the earth to express the adorable perfection of God the Father in a tangible way. In his person alone, he bore the beauties of God the Father, his purity and love, his wisdom and prudence, his mercy and compassion. One saint alone is destined to represent God the Father while an infinite number of creatures, a multitude of saints are needed to represent Jesus ... Hence, the majestic St. Joseph must be considered as the greatest, the most famous and the most incomprehensible person in the world. The Father, having chosen this saint to make of him his image on earth."

Monsignor Jean Jacques Olier
Saint Joseph: Shadow of the Father, p. 51

A Light for our Homes

"How much the family of today can learn from this! 'The essence and role of the family are in the final analysis specified by love ... This being the case, it is in the Holy Family, the original 'Church in miniature (*Ecclesia Domestica*), that every Christian family must be reflected. 'Through God's mysterious design, it was in that family that the Son of God spent long years of a hidden life. It is therefore the prototype and example for all Christian families.'"

St. John Paul II, *Redemptoris Custos*, #7

The Mystery of the Home

- "For by His incarnation the Son of God has united Himself in some fashion with every man" (Second Vatican Council, *Gaudium et Spes*, #22).

- "Each and every time that motherhood is repeated in human history, it is always related to the Covenant which God established with the human race through the motherhood of the mother of God" (St. Pope John Paul II, *Mulieris Dignitatem*, #11).

- "Men relive and reveal on earth the very fatherhood of God" (St. Pope John Paul II, *Familiaris Consortio*, #25).

The Universal Call to Holiness

"Everyone whether belonging to the hierarchy, or being cared for by it, is called to holiness, according to the saying of the Apostle: 'For this is the will of God, your sanctification' (1 Thessalonians 2:4). However, this holiness of the Church is ... expressed in many ways in individuals, who in their walk of life, tend toward the perfection of charity."

Lumen Gentium, #39

The Pathway to Holiness

- "Holy Baptism is the basis of the whole Christian life, the gateway to life in the Spirit" (Catechism #1213).

- "The sacrament of marriage ... takes up again and makes specific the sanctifying grace of Baptism." "Spouses participate in [the event of salvation] as spouses, together as a couple, so that the first and immediate effect of marriage is ... the Christian conjugal bond" (Pope John Paul II, *Familiaris Consortio*, #56 and #13)

Everyone is called to become holy in their state-in-life. The vast majority of men in That Man is You! are husbands and fathers. Some men will experience "a call within a call."

The Call to Mission

"The Christ whom we have contemplated and loved bids us to set out once more on our journey: 'Go therefore and make disciples of all nations, baptizing them in the name of the Father, and of the Son and of the Holy Spirit' (Matthew 28:19). The missionary mandate accompanies us into the Third Millennium and urges us to share the enthusiasm of the very first Christians."

Pope John Paul II
Novo Millennio Ineunte, #58

A Special Mission to Families

"But it is especially necessary to recognize the unique place that, in this field, belongs to the mission of married couples and Christian families, by virtue of the grace received in the sacrament ... Christ confers upon Christian married couples a special "mission as apostles, sending them as workers into His vineyard, and, in a very special way, into this field of the family."

Pope John Paul II
Familiaris Consortio, #71

A Call to be a Spiritual Mentor

- TMIY Buddy System: "Two are better than one ... if they fall, one will lift up his fellow, but woe to him who is alone when he falls and has not another to lift him up" (Ecclesiastes 4:9-10).

- "Whoever brings back a sinner from the error of his way will save his soul from death and will cover a multitude of sins" (James 5:20).

- "Let not many of you become teachers, my brethren, for you know that we who teach shall be judged with greater strictness" (James 3:1).

Practical Recommendations

- Pray for the grace to become holy as a husband and father.
- Profoundly live the 7 Covenants of TMIY.
- Learn the principles of the TMIY App.
- Be docile for a call to help other families tread the path to Nazareth.
- Contact TMIY if you think you have received a call to become a spiritual mentor for other TMIY men.

"A call within a call" must always remain faithful to the first call. The vast majority of men in That Man is You! will tread the path to heaven as husbands and fathers.

Small Group Discussion

Starter Questions

1. How can you become holy as a husband and father?
2. Do you perceive a call to become an apostle to the family? How can you fulfill this call?

Next Week
Reading Signs from God

SESSION 22

Reading Signs from God

TMIY
THAT MAN IS YOU!
BECOMING A MAN AFTER GOD'S OWN HEART

Believe it or not, next week is Holy Week. Let us endeavor to follow Christ to the end.

Entry into the Spirit of Nazareth

- "O Mary Immaculate, O glorious Joseph! And you, St. John, beloved disciple of the Divine Heart, teach me the great science of love" (St. Bernadette).

- "The Church must make this journey, which takes her from the temple she has built for herself to this house that God makes for her … that is, to true interior life, the life of the Holy Family … Mary makes Christians take the road to the Holy Family, where the Gospel is lived in its plenitude" (Fr. Andrew Doze).

Source: Doze, Fr. Andrew, "Saint Joseph: The Shadow of the Father," Trans. Andett, F., Alba House, New York, 1992, p. 63 and pp. 72-73.

The Daily Lenten Program

1. Begin the day with a consecration of the day and ourselves to Our Lady.

2. Daily Lectio Divina using Scriptural passages and meditation starters.

3. Recitation of the Most Holy Rosary of the Blessed Virgin Mary.

4. Brief examination of conscience at the end of the day.

The Weekly Lenten Program

1. Discernment at Nazareth
   - External Signs from God
2. Practical Recommendation
   - Pray. Pray. Pray.
   - Do NOT demand signs. Allow God to send them to you spontaneously.
   - Realize God will always require you to act in faith.
   - Remain open to God's continued guidance.

The Spirit of Nazareth
BY STEVE BOLLMANN

St. Joseph at Nazareth

1. Divine Dialogue
2. Our Lady
3. Silence
4. Obedience to God's Representatives
5. Fidelity to State-in-Life
6. External Signs
7. Peace

{ Create Nazareth within our hearts.

{ Discern the movement of the Holy Spirit in our hearts.

The Spirit of Nazareth
BY STEVE BOLLMANN

The Call of the Holy Family

"In the sixth month the angel Gabriel was sent from God to a city of Galilee named Nazareth, to a virgin betrothed to a man whose name was Joseph ... The angel Gabriel said: 'Hail, full of grace, the Lord is with you ... you will conceive in your womb and bear a son, and you will call his name Jesus ... He will be called the Son of the Most High ... The Holy Spirit will come upon you and the power of the Most High will overshadow you; therefore the child to be born will be called holy, the Son of God.

Luke 1:26-38

Our Lady and St. Joseph had greater faith than anyone else either before or after them.

Nonetheless, God was willing to help their faith with signs from heaven.

A Sign from God

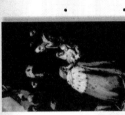

"Behold, your kinswoman Elizabeth in her old age has also conceived a son; and this is the sixth month with her who was called barren. For with God nothing will be impossible."

Luke 1:36-37

Confirmation from God

- "In that region there were shepherds out in the field ... suddenly there was with the angel a multitude of the heavenly host praising God and ... they went with haste and found Mary and Joseph, and ... they made known the saying which had been told them concerning the child" (Luke 2:8-18).

- "Going into the house they saw the child with Mary his mother, and they fell down and worshiped him. Then, opening their treasures, they offered him gifts, gold and frankincense and myrrh" (Matthew 2:11).

- "There was a man in Jerusalem, whose name was Simeon ... he took [the baby] up in his arms and blessed God and said ... 'mine eyes have seen thy salvation'" (Luke 2:22-35).

The Conversion of St. Paul

"As Paul journeyed he approached Damascus, and suddenly a light from heaven flashed about him. And he fell to the ground and heard a voice saying to him, 'Saul, Saul, why do you persecute me?' And he said, 'Who are you, Lord?' And he said, 'I am Jesus, whom you are persecuting; but rise and enter the city, and you will be told what you are to do.' ... Saul arose from the ground; and when his eyes were opened, he could see nothing; so they led him by the hand and brought him into Damascus."

Acts 9:1-9

✝ As we seek to fulfill God's will in our life, he will give us signs to help guide us along the way. ✝

A Messenger from God

"The Lord said to Ananias, 'Rise … and inquire in the house of Judas for a man of Tarsus named Saul … for he is a chosen instrument of mine to carry my name before the Gentiles and kings and the sons of Israel' … Ananias said, 'Brother Saul, the Lord Jesus … has sent me that you may regain your sight and be filled with the Holy Spirit.' And immediately something like scales fell from his eyes and he regained his sight. Then he rose and was baptized, and took food and was strengthened."

Acts 9:10-19

Guidance from God

"Almost the whole city gathered to hear the word of God. When the Jews saw the multitudes, they were filled with jealousy, and contradicted what was spoken by Paul, and reviled him. Paul and Barnabas spoke out boldly, saying, 'It was necessary that the word of God should be spoken first to you. Since you thrust it from you, and judge yourselves unworthy of eternal life, behold, we turn to the Gentiles. For so the Lord has commanded us, saying, 'I have set you to be a light for the Gentiles.''"

Acts 13:41-42

Redirected by God

"They went through the region of Phrygia and Galatia, having been forbidden by the Holy Spirit to speak the word in Asia … they attempted to go into Bithynia, but the Spirit of Jesus did not allow them … And a vision appeared to Paul in the night: a man of Macedonia was standing beseeching him and saying, 'Come over to Macedonia and help us.' And when he had seen the vision, immediately we sought to go on into Macedonia, concluding that God had called us to preach the gospel to them."

Acts 16:1-10

Fruitfulness in God

"I am the vine, you are the branches. He who abides in me, and I in him, he it is that bears much fruit, for apart from me you can do nothing … By this my Father is glorified, that you bear much fruit, and so prove to be my disciples." "Thus you will know them by their fruits."

John 15:1-8/Matthew 7:20

A Great Sign in Heaven

"And a great sign appeared in heaven, a woman clothed with the sun, with the moon under her feet, and on her head a crown of twelve stars; she was with child and she cried out in her pangs of birth, in anguish for delivery. And another sign appeared in heaven; behold, a great red dragon ... stood before the woman who was about to bear a child ... but her child was caught up to God .... Now war arose in heaven, Michael and his angels fighting against the dragon; and the dragon and his angels fought, but they were defeated and there was no longer place for them in heaven."

Revelation 12:1-8

Is God sending the world any signs today?

Yes.

It is a sign in the heavens!

The Apparition of Our Lady at Lourdes

- Our Lady makes 18 apparitions to Bernadette Soubirous between February 11-July 16, 1858.
  - Feb 25th – the Spring of Lourdes is revealed: "Go and drink at the spring and wash yourself in it."
  - Mar 2nd – "Go and tell the priests that people are to come here in procession and to build a chapel here."
- "Mary makes Bernadette enter into the particularly special atmosphere of the family ... Mary makes the Christians take the road to the Holy Family, where the Gospel is lived in its plentitude" (Fr. Andrew Doze).

Source: Laurentin, R., "Bernadette of Lourdes," Duxton, Longman and Todd, Ltd, 1999.
Sanctuary of Our Lady of Lourdes website,
www.en.lourdes-france.org
Doze, Fr. Andrew, "Saint Joseph: The Shadow of the Father," Trans. Andert, F., Alba House, 1992.

The Miraculous Medal Apparition

- "Come to the foot of the altar. There graces will be shed upon all, great and little, who ask for them" (July 18, 1830).
- "[Mary's] arms swept wide in a gesture of motherly compassion, while from her jeweled fingers the rays of light streamed upon the white globe at her feet. An oval formed around the Blessed Virgin: 'O Mary, conceived without sin, pray for us who have recourse to thee.' Have a medal struck after this model. All who wear it will receive great graces. They should wear it around the neck. Graces will abound for persons who wear it with confidence" (November 27, 1830).

Source: Darvin, J., "Saint Catherine Labouré of the Miraculous Medal," Tan Books and Publishers, 1984.

St. Pope John Paul II specifically related these apparitions to the vision of the "woman clothed with the sun."

Pope Pius XII called it "an incomparable outpouring of the grace of redemption."

The Vision of the Holy Family

- "'Continue always to pray the Rosary every day' … Then, opening her hands, she made them reflect on the sun, and as she ascended, the reflection of her own light continued to be projected on the sun itself … After Our Lady had disappeared into the immense distance of the firmament, we beheld St. Joseph with the Child Jesus and Our Lady robed in white with a blue mantle, beside the sun. St. Joseph and the Child Jesus appeared to bless the world, for they traced the Sign of the Cross with their hands" (October 13, 1917).

- "I shall come to ask for the consecration of Russia to my Immaculate Heart , and the Communion of reparation on the First Saturdays" (July 13, 1917).

Source: "Fatima in Lucia's own Words," edited by Fr. Louis Kondor, SVD, The Ravengate Press, 1989, pp. 169-170 and 104.

Small Group Discussion

Starter Questions

1. How is God speaking to you through external signs?
2. How are you going to make sure that the signs are from God and leading you to him?

Next Week
A Peace not of this World

Practical Recommendations

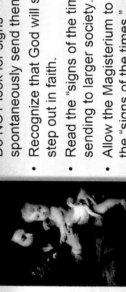

- Do NOT look for signs – let God spontaneously send them to you.

- Recognize that God will still require you to step out in faith.

- Read the "signs of the times" that God is sending to larger society.

- Allow the Magisterium to guide you in reading the "signs of the times."

SESSION 23

A Peace not of this World

TMIY

THAT MAN IS YOU!

BECOMING A MAN AFTER GOD'S OWN HEART

It is Holy Week. Let us remain united to Christ and listen to his "still, small voice."

Entry into the Spirit of Nazareth

- "O Mary Immaculate, O glorious Joseph! And you, St. John, beloved disciple of the Divine Heart, teach me the great science of love" (St. Bernadette).

- "The Church must make this journey, which takes her from the temple she has built for herself to this house that God makes for her … that is, to true interior life, the life of the Holy Family … Mary makes Christians take the road to the Holy Family, where the Gospel is lived in its plenitude" (Fr. Andrew Doze).

Source: Doze, Fr. Andrew, "Saint Joseph: The Shadow of the Father," Trans. Audett, Fr. Albn House, New York, 1992, p. 68 and pp. 72-73.

The Daily Lenten Program

The Spirit of Nazareth

A Lenten Journey for Men

BY STEVE BOLLMAN

1. Begin the day with a consecration of the day and ourselves to Our Lady.

2. Daily Lectio Divina using Scriptural passages and meditation starters.

3. Recitation of the Most Holy Rosary of the Blessed Virgin Mary.

4. Brief examination of conscience at the end of the day.

The Weekly Lenten Program

1. Discernment at Nazareth
   - The gift of peace.
2. Practical Recommendation
   - Follow the seven steps for discerning God's will in your life.

Peace in the Garden of Eden

- "Therefore a man leaves his father and his mother and cleaves to his wife, and they become one flesh. And the man and his wife were both naked, and were not ashamed" (Genesis 2:24-25).
- "They knew that they were naked; and they sewed fig leaves together and made themselves aprons ... 'Your desire shall be for your husband, and he shall rule over you'" (Genesis 3:7-16).

St. Joseph at Nazareth

1. Divine Dialogue
2. Our Lady
3. Silence   } Create Nazareth within our hearts.
4. Obedience to God's Representatives
5. Fidelity to State-in-Life   } Discern the movement of the Holy Spirit in our hearts.
6. External Signs
7. Peace

Peace is very important in the spiritual life and in discerning God's will in your life. Peace is a gift from God.

The Gift of Peace

"On the evening of the first day of the week ... Jesus came and stood among the disciples and ... said to them again, 'Peace be with you. As the Father has sent me, even so I send you.' And when he had said this, he breathed on them, and said to them, 'Receive the Holy Spirit.'"

John 20:19-23

If peace is a sign of God's presence and kingdom, let us consider peace within the context of the Holy Family.

The Holy Family was a heaven, a paradise on earth, endless delights in this place of grief; it was a glory already begun in the vileness, abjection and lowliness of their life.

Monsignor Jean Jacques Olier

Source: Doze, Fr. Andrew. "Saint Joseph; The Shadow of the Father," Trans. Audet, F., Alba House, New York, 1992, p. 52.

Trial at the Annunciation

"In the sixth month the angel Gabriel was sent from God to a city of Galilee named Nazareth, to a virgin betrothed to a man whose name was Joseph ... And he came to her and said, 'Hail, full of grace, the Lord is with you!' But she was greatly troubled at the saying, and considered in her mind what sort of greeting this might be" (Luke 1:26-29).

"Her husband Joseph, being a just man and unwilling to put her to shame, resolved to send her away quietly. But as he considered this, behold, an angel of the Lord appeared to him in a dream, saying, 'Joseph, son of David, do not fear to take Mary your wife" (Matthew 1:18-20).

Trial at the Birth

"In those days a decree went out from Caesar Augustus that all the world should be enrolled ... And all went to be enrolled, each to his own city. And Joseph also went up fro Galilee, to the city of David, which is called Bethlehem, because he was of the house and lineage of David, to be enrolled with Mary his betrothed, who was with child. And while they were there, the time came for her to be delivered. And she gave birth to her first-born son and wrapped him in swaddling cloths, and laid him in a manger, because there was no place for them in the inn."

Luke 2:1-7

Trial during Christ's Childhood

"When Jesus was twelve years old, they went up according to custom ... as they were returning, the boy Jesus stayed behind in Jerusalem. His parents did not know it, but supposing him to be in the company they went a day's journey ... when they did not find him, they returned to Jerusalem, seeking him. After three days they found him in the temple, sitting among the teachers, listening to them and asking them questions ... and when they saw him they were astonished; and his mother said to him, 'Son, why have you treated us so? Behold, your father and I have been looking for you anxiously.'"

Luke 2:39-48

Peace not of This World

- "Peace I leave with you; my peace I give to you; not as the world gives do I give to you. Let not your hearts be troubled, neither let them be afraid ... for the ruler of this world is coming. He has no power over me" (John 14:27-30).

- "Have no anxiety about anything, but in everything by prayer and supplication with thanksgiving let your requests be made known to God. And the peace of God, which passes all understanding, will keep your hearts and your minds in Christ Jesus" (Philippians 4:6-7).

✠ The Holy Family experienced great struggle. The peace of Christ must look different from the peace of the world.

✠

Peace in the Midst of Torment

"Jesus knelt down and prayed, 'Father, if thou art willing, remove this cup from me; nevertheless not my will, but thine be done.' And there appeared to him an angel from heaven, strengthening him. And being in an agony he prayed more earnestly; and his sweat became like great drops of blood falling down upon the ground."

Luke 22:41-44

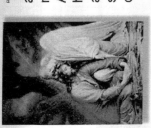

Source: "Fatima in Lucia's own Words," edited by Fr. Louis Kondor, SVD, The Ravengate Press, 1989, pp. 104-105

The possibility to experience peace in the midst of great difficulties is very important. Our world is beset by difficulties.

The Promise of Peace

"You have seen hell where the souls of poor sinners go. To save them, God wishes to establish in the world devotion to my Immaculate Heart ... When you see a night illumined by an unknown light, know that this is the great sign given you by God that He is about to punish the world for its crimes, by means of war, famine, and persecutions of the Church and of the Holy Father ... Russia will spread her errors throughout the world, causing wars and persecutions of the Church. The good will be martyred; the Holy Father will have much to suffer; various nations will be annihilated. In the end, my Immaculate Heart will triumph ... and a period of peace will be granted to the world" (July 13, 1917).

Builders of a Civilization of Love

"The aspiration that humanity nurtures, amid countless injustices and sufferings, is the hope of a new civilization marked by freedom and peace. But for such an undertaking, a new generation of builders is needed ... You are the men and women of tomorrow. The future is in your hearts and in your hands. God is entrusting to you the task, at once difficult and uplifting, of working with him in the building of the civilization of love."

Pope John Paul II
Evening Vigil with Young People, #4
World Youth Day, Toronto, 2002
Downsview Park, Saturday 27, 200

The Seven Principles to Discern Holy Desires

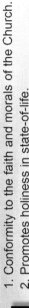

1. Conformity to the faith and morals of the Church.
2. Promotes holiness in state-of-life.
3. Occurs without cause of through the soul's own acts of will or intellect.
4. Establishes and/or promotes peace, tranquility and quiet vs. hinders and/or destroys the same qualities.
5. Subtleness/gentleness vs. agitation of movement.
6. Proximity to onset of movement.
7. External validation.

Small Group Discussion

Starter Questions

1. How are you going to make discernment part of your spiritual life and who is going to help you?
2. What holy desires do you have in your heart?

Next Week

The Vineyard of the Family

The Church is heading into a new springtime. It is a period of peace.

Have you received a "call within a call" to help build this new springtime?

You need to discern carefully.

CERTIFICATE OF RECOGNITION

SESSION 24

The Vineyard of the Family

TMIY

THAT MAN IS YOU!

BECOMING A MAN AFTER GOD'S OWN HEART

The Church is heading into a new springtime.

"The harvest is plentiful, but the laborers are few; pray therefore the Lord of the harvest to send out laborers into his harvest" (Luke 10:2).

A New Springtime for Christianity

- "I see the dawning of a new missionary age, which will become a radiant day bearing an abundant harvest.... As the third millennium of the redemption draws near, God is preparing a great springtime for Christianity" (Pope John Paul II, *Redemptoris Missio*, #92 and #86).

- "I understood that I must lead Christ's Church into this third millennium through suffering ... Precisely because the family is threatened, the family is under attack. The Pope has to be attacked, the Pope has to suffer, so that every family and the world may see that there is ... a higher Gospel ... by which the future is prepared, the third millennium of families" (May 29, 1994).

Builders of a Civilization of Love

"The aspiration that humanity nurtures, amid countless injustices and sufferings, is the hope of a new civilization marked by freedom and peace. But for such an undertaking, a new generation of builders is needed ... You are the men and women of tomorrow. The future is in your hearts and in your hands. God is entrusting to you the task, at once difficult and uplifting, of working with him in the building of the civilization of love."

Pope John Paul II
Evening Vigil with Young People, #4
World Youth Day, Toronto, 2002
Downsview Park, Saturday 27, 200

Apostles to the Family

"It is especially necessary to recognize the unique place that ... belongs to the mission of married couples and Christian families, by virtue of the grace received in the sacrament. This mission must be placed at the service of the building up of the Kingdom of God in history. This is demanded as an act of docile obedience to Christ the Lord. For it is He who, by virtue of the fact that marriage of baptized persons has been raised to a sacrament, confers upon Christian married couples a special mission as apostle, sending them as workers into His vineyard, and, in a very special way, into this field of the family."

Pope John Paul II
Familiaris Consortio, #71

I know that God called me.

I have tried to answer that call.

Has God called you?

There are four dimensions to the call.

You may be called to embrace some or all.

To Live It is the most important and foundation.

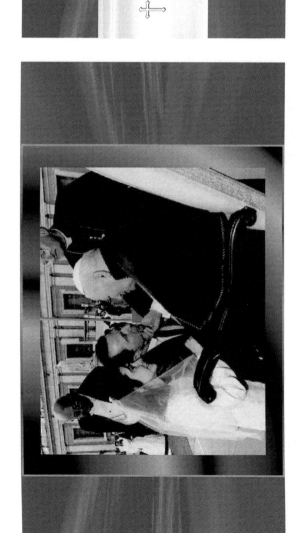

A Call to Live It

Embrace the 7 Steps as a Pathway to Holiness

1. Daily
   - Live the "Spirit of Nazareth" by using the 7 Steps as the organizing principle of spiritual life.
   - Consecrate day to Our Lady/Recite Paradisus Dei's "Apostles of a New Springtime" Prayer.
   - Morning Prayer
   - Evening or Night Prayer
   - Rosary: "If you want peace to reign in your home, say the beads there, every day, with your family" (Pope St. Pius X).
   - Scripture (during Morning or Night Prayer)
   - Examine (during Night Prayer)

A Call to Live It

Embrace the 7 Steps as a Pathway to Holiness

2. Weekly
   - Attend Mass at least one day in addition to Sunday.
   - Gather with other TMIY men and/or Paradisus Dei individuals or couples to discuss living the 7 Steps as a pathway to holiness.
   - When a group gathering is not possible, have a "spiritual conversation" with at least one other person embracing the 7 Steps.

A Call to Live It

Embrace the 7 Steps as a Pathway to Holiness

3. Monthly
   - Practice the First Friday Devotion to the Sacred Heart: "I promise you in the excessive mercy of My Heart that Its all-powerful love will grant to all those who receive Holy Communion on nine first Fridays of the month consecutively, that grace of final repentance."
   - Includes Mass.
   - Includes Confession (at least one week before or after the First Friday).
   - Gather with other Paradisus Dei individuals for fellowship and formation.

A Call to Live It

Embrace the 7 Steps as a Pathway to Holiness

4. Annual
   - Review Spiritual Plan of Life and Apostolic activities during a TMIY "12 Day Novena."
   - Don Bosco (Jan. 31) – Our Lady of Lourdes (Feb. 11).
   - Miraculous Medal (Nov. 27) – Immaculate Conception (Dec. 8).
   - Celebrate the Feast of Our Lady of Lourdes with other Paradisus Dei individuals.

A Call to Live It

Beyond live it, some are called to:

Share it. Spread it. Fund it.

A Call to Live It

THAT MAN IS YOU!™
BECOMING A MAN AFTER GOD'S OWN HEART

Embrace the 7 Steps as a Pathway to Holiness

5. Lifetime

- Make a pilgrimage to a Holy Site – preferably one associated with the Holy Family in some way.
- Paradisus Dei leads international pilgrimages to Rome, Lourdes, Holy Land.
- Paradisus Dei coordinates domestic pilgrimages.
- Can be fulfilled in every diocese.

A Call to Spread It

THAT MAN IS YOU!™
BECOMING A MAN AFTER GOD'S OWN HEART

1. Willingness to help spread TMIY and Paradisus Dei programming on a local, diocesan and national level.
2. Willingness to participate in a Mission Apostle Group (MAG) to help spread TMIY within your diocese.
3. Willingness to use appropriate technology and marketing to spread TMIY.

A Call to Share It

THAT MAN IS YOU!™
BECOMING A MAN AFTER GOD'S OWN HEART

1. Willingness to live the 7 Steps to an eminent degree.
2. Willingness to share within one's everyday acquaintances the power of the 7 Steps.
3. Willingness to help others live the 7 Steps.
4. Willingness to receive special training to become a spiritual mentor in your TMIY community.

A Call to Fund It

1. Willingness to donate and help raise funds necessary to help make Paradisus Dei programs available to parishes and individuals who could not afford them.

2. Giving Societies:
   - St. Michael the Archangel – sponsor Paradisus Dei programming to larger community.
   - St. Rafael the Archangel – sponsor Paradisus Dei materials to youth, engaged and newlywed couples.
   - St. Gabriel the Archangel – help underwrite the production of Paradisus Dei materials.

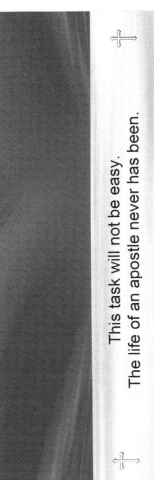

This task will not be easy.

The life of an apostle never has been.

The Challenges of an Apostle

"One man, one woman in a permanent, exclusive union open to life."

- Monogamous: only 186 of 1231 cultures dating back to the 8th Century B.C. were monogamous.
- Permanent: Forty percent of marriages in the United States end in divorce – most Christian denominations don't teach.
- Exclusive: Two-thirds of youth cohabitate; 10% are virgins at time of marriage, 25% have an extramarital affair; 70% of men visit a porn site every month.
- Open to life: 98% of women use contraception at some point in their reproductive life; Two-thirds of couples in 40-44 age group have one partner sterilized.

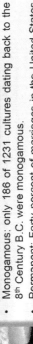

Crossing the Threshold of Hope

"Now is the time for hope ... We must not be afraid of the future. We must not be afraid of man ... Each and every human person has been created in the 'image and likeness' of the One who is the origin of all that is ... with the help of God's grace, we can build in the next century and the next millennium a civilization worthy of the human person ... And in doing so, we shall see that the tears of this century have prepared the ground for a new springtime of the human spirit."

St. John Paul II
United Nations
October 5, 1995

Answering the Call

1. Every man who has a holy desire in his heart to help in this mission, please stand.

2. Together we will recite Paradisus Dei's prayer: Apostles of a New Springtime.

3. Individual men will then sign their name and indicate their call (live, share, spread, fund) on the form at the front.

4. The Core Team Leader will then place a Miraculous Medal around your neck.

5. A Core Team member will sign and hand you your certificate.

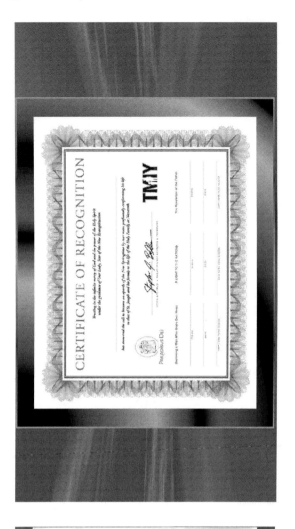

Small Group Discussion

Starter Questions

1. What holy desire do you have in your heart? What call have you received?
2. How are you going to fulfill this call and desire?

Next Year
A Light to the Nations

The Mission of Apostle

"'Go and make disciples of all the nations.' With these words, Jesus is speaking to each one of us saying: '... now you must go, now you must pass on this experience to others' ... Jesus did not say: 'Go, if you would like to, if you have the time'; but he said: "Go and make disciples of all nations.' Sharing the experience of faith, bearing witness to the faith, proclaiming the Gospel: this is a command that the Lord entrusts to the whole Church, and that includes you ... Some people might think: 'I have no particular preparation, how can I go and proclaim the Gospel?' ... God says the same thing to you as he said to Jeremiah: 'Be not afraid ... for I am with you to deliver you' (Jeremiah 1:7-8)."

Pope Francis
World Youth Day, Rio de Janeiro
July 28, 2013

Made in the USA
San Bernardino, CA
30 October 2015